Crafting for Sι

Essential Guide Which Will Help y
Worst-Case Scenario
Mike Sheffield

Table of Content
I. Introduction

- Explanation of the purpose of the book
- Overview of the topics that will be covered

II. Basic Survival Skills

- Building shelter
- Finding and purifying water
- Starting a fire
- Foraging for food
- Navigation and orienteering

III. Crafting for Survival

- Making tools and weapons
- Building traps and snares
- Creating clothing and footwear
- Building and maintaining equipment
- Improvised medical treatments

IV. Conclusion

- Summary of key takeaways
- Resources for further learning and practice

V. Appendices

- List of materials and equipment needed for survival crafting
- Examples of specific survival scenarios and how to prepare for them
- Glossary of terms used in the book

© **Copyright. All rights reserved. Mike Sheffield**

The content contained within this book may not be reproduced, duplicated or transmitted without direct written permission from the author or the publisher.

Under no circumstances will any blame or legal responsibility be held against the publisher, or author, for any damages, reparation, or monetary loss due to the information contained within this book. Either directly or indirectly.

Legal Notice:

This book is copyright protected. This book is only for personal use. You cannot amend, distribute, sell, use, quote or paraphrase any part, or the content within this book, without the consent of the author or publisher.

Disclaimer Notice:

Please note the information contained within this document is for educational and entertainment purposes only. All effort has been executed to present accurate, up to date, and reliable, complete information. No warranties of any kind are declared or implied. Readers acknowledge that the author is not engaging in the rendering of legal, financial, medical or professional advice. The content within this book has been derived from various sources. Please consult a licensed professional before attempting any techniques outlined in this book.

By reading this document, the reader agrees that under no circumstances is the author responsible for any losses, direct or indirect, which are incurred as a result of the use of information contained within this document, including, but not limited to, — errors, omissions, or inaccuracies.

I. Introduction

- **Explanation of the purpose of the book**

The purpose of this book, "Crafting for Survival: Essential Guide" is to provide readers with the knowledge and skills needed to survive in any worst-case scenario. The book covers a wide range of topics, including basic survival skills, crafting techniques, and advanced survival strategies. It is designed to be a comprehensive guide, providing readers with everything they need to know to stay alive and thrive in challenging situations, whether they are stranded in the wilderness, dealing with a natural disaster, or facing other types of emergencies. The book is intended for anyone who is interested in survival and preparedness, from outdoor enthusiasts to preppers, and will provide readers with the tools and knowledge they need to survive and thrive in any situation.

- **Overview of the topics that will be covered**

The book will cover a wide range of topics related to survival crafting, including:

- Basic survival skills such as building shelter, finding and purifying water, starting a fire, foraging for food, and navigation and orienteering.
- Techniques for crafting essential items for survival such as tools and weapons, traps and snares, clothing and footwear, and equipment.
- Advanced survival techniques such as surviving in extreme environments, dealing with natural disasters, surviving in urban environments, and long-term survival strategies.
- The creation and use of bug-out bags and survival kits.
- The book will also provide appendices that include a list of materials and equipment needed for survival crafting, examples of specific survival scenarios and how to prepare for them, glossary of terms used in the book, and additional reading and references.

II. Basic Survival Skills

- **Building shelter**

Building Shelter
Building a shelter is one of the most critical survival skills that you need to master. It is essential for protecting yourself from the elements, providing a safe place to sleep, and helping you to maintain your body temperature. In this chapter, we will cover various shelter-building techniques that you can use in different environments and situations.

Section 1: Natural Shelters

- Building a shelter using natural materials such as branches, leaves, and rocks

Building a shelter using natural materials is an essential survival skill that can help protect you from the elements and improve your chances of survival in an emergency situation. Here is a guide on how to build a shelter using natural materials such as branches, leaves, and rocks.

Materials:

- Branches (for the frame)
- Leaves or grass (for the roof)
- Rocks (for securing the shelter)
- Rope or cordage (for tying the shelter together)
- A tarp or plastic sheet (for extra waterproofing)

Step 1: Choose a location Select a location for your shelter that is protected from the wind and rain, and preferably close to a water source. A slope or a small hill can be a good location, as it will provide natural drainage for water. Make sure the location is clear of any potential hazards, such as poisonous plants or dangerous animals.

Step 2: Gather materials Collect branches, leaves, and rocks in the area. The branches should be sturdy enough to support the weight of the roof, and the leaves or grass should be dry and free from mold or mildew. The rocks should be large enough to hold down the shelter and prevent it from blowing away.

Step 3: Build the frame Using the branches, create a frame for the shelter. Start by leaning two branches against each other at a slight angle, then tie them together at the top with rope or cordage. Repeat this process, creating a frame that is roughly the shape of a triangle. Be sure to make the frame as stable as possible, and make sure the shelter is big enough to fit you comfortably.

Step 4: Add the roof Cover the frame with leaves or grass, layering them until the roof is thick enough to provide adequate protection from the elements. If you have a tarp or plastic sheet, you can use it to cover the roof for extra waterproofing.

Step 5: Secure the shelter Use the rocks to hold down the shelter and prevent it from blowing away. Place the rocks around the base of the shelter, and at the corners to make sure the shelter is stable.

Step 6: Final touches Finally, add any other materials you have to make the shelter more comfortable, such as a bed of leaves or grass to sleep on.

Building a shelter can take time and practice, but with the right materials and techniques, you can create a shelter that will protect you from the elements and improve your chances of survival in an emergency situation. Remember to always be aware of your surroundings and the potential hazards, and never put yourself in a dangerous situation.

- Finding and using caves and overhangs

Caves and overhangs can provide natural shelter and protection from the elements, making them an excellent survival resource. Here is a guide on how to find and use caves and overhangs for survival.

Step 1: Look for signs of caves and overhangs When looking for caves and overhangs, pay attention to the terrain. Caves are often found in areas with limestone or sandstone, and may be hidden behind bushes or trees. Overhangs can be found in areas with steep cliffs or rocky outcroppings. Look for shadows, crevices, and openings in the rocks.

Step 2: Approach with caution When you have located a cave or overhang, approach with caution. Caves can be home to dangerous animals, such as bats or bears, and overhangs may be unstable. Make sure to bring a flashlight or a headlamp, and always have a way to defend yourself if necessary.

Step 3: Check for hazards Before entering a cave or overhang, check for hazards. Look for signs of recent animal activity, such as droppings or tracks, and make sure there are no dangerous creatures inside. Check the roof and walls for signs of instability, such as cracks or loose rocks, and make sure the cave is not prone to flooding.

Step 4: Make a fire If it is safe to do so, start a fire inside the cave or overhang. Not only will this provide warmth and light, but it will also help to keep animals away. Make sure to build the fire on a level surface and use fire-resistant materials, such as rocks or sand, to contain the fire.

Step 5: Use the cave or overhang as a base Caves and overhangs can provide a great base for survival. They can be used to store supplies, cook food, and rest. Keep in mind that caves can get very cold at night, so be sure to bring warm clothing, and always have a way to make a fire.

- Building a shelter using a tarp or plastic sheeting

Building a shelter using a tarp or plastic sheeting is a quick and easy way to provide protection from the elements. Here is a guide on how to build a shelter using a tarp or plastic sheeting.

Step 1: Gather materials You will need a tarp or plastic sheeting, some rope or paracord, and some sturdy branches or poles. Make sure the tarp or plastic sheeting is large enough to cover the area you want to shelter.

Step 2: Choose a location Choose a location for your shelter that is flat and dry, with good drainage. Avoid low-lying areas where water may collect, and make sure the area is clear of debris and hazards.

Step 3: Set up the frame Use the branches or poles to create a frame for your shelter. You can use a variety of different frame designs depending on the materials you have available and the conditions you are facing. Some popular designs include the A-frame, the lean-to, and the teepee. Make sure the frame is sturdy and secure.

Step 4: Attach the tarp or plastic sheeting Once the frame is set up, drape the tarp or plastic sheeting over it, making sure it covers the entire frame. Use the rope or paracord to secure the tarp or plastic sheeting to the frame. Make sure the tarp or plastic sheeting is tight and secure, with no wrinkles or folds that may collect water.

Step 5: Secure the shelter Use additional rope or paracord to secure the shelter to the ground. Make sure the shelter is stable and secure, and that it won't collapse in high winds or heavy rain.

Step 6: Add additional features You can add additional features to your shelter such as a door, a window, or a ventilation system. You can also add insulation by using natural materials such as leaves or moss, or by adding an additional layer of tarp or plastic sheeting.

Section 2: Improvised Shelters

- Building a shelter using a space blanket

Building a shelter using a space blanket is a quick and easy way to protect yourself from the elements in an emergency situation. Here is a step-by-step guide on how to do it:

1. Find a flat, open area to build your shelter. Look for a spot that is protected from the wind and has a solid surface to anchor the blanket to.
2. Lay the space blanket out on the ground, shiny side up. Make sure it is fully opened and stretched out.
3. Secure the corners of the blanket to the ground using rocks, branches, or other heavy objects. This will keep the blanket in place and prevent it from blowing away.
4. Use branches, poles, or other long, sturdy objects to create a frame for your shelter. Place them in a teepee shape over the blanket, making sure they are securely anchored to the ground.
5. Cover the frame with the space blanket, tucking the edges under the branches or poles to secure it in place.
6. Use additional branches or other materials to create a door for your shelter. This will help keep out the wind and provide some privacy.
7. Insulate the floor by spreading leaves, moss, or other soft materials on the ground inside the shelter.
8. Make sure to check your shelter frequently, and make adjustments as needed to keep it secure and functional.

Note: Space blanket is not a long term solution and should be used in emergency only.

- Building a shelter using a garbage bag

Building a shelter using a garbage bag can be a quick and easy way to protect yourself from the elements in an emergency situation. However, it is important to note that a garbage bag shelter should only be used as a temporary solution, as it is not designed for long-term use.

Here is a step-by-step guide on how to build a shelter using a garbage bag:

1. Find a flat, open area to build your shelter. Look for a spot that is protected from the wind and has a solid surface to anchor the bag to.
2. Lay the garbage bag out on the ground, with the open end facing up.
3. Use branches, poles, or other long, sturdy objects to create a frame for your shelter. Place them in a teepee shape over the bag, making sure they are securely anchored to the ground.
4. Cover the frame with the garbage bag, tucking the edges under the branches or poles to secure it in place.
5. Use additional branches or other materials to create a door for your shelter. This will help keep out the wind and provide some privacy.
6. Insulate the floor by spreading leaves, moss, or other soft materials on the ground inside the shelter.
7. Make sure to check your shelter frequently, and make adjustments as needed to keep it secure and functional.

It is important to note that a garbage bag shelter is not a suitable long-term solution, as it is not designed to withstand heavy rain or strong winds. It is best used as a temporary shelter in an emergency situation. Always keep in mind that safety is most important and always try to find a better solution if possible.

- Building a shelter using a poncho

Building a shelter using a poncho can be a quick and easy way to protect yourself from the elements in an emergency situation. However, it is important to note that a poncho shelter should only be used as a temporary solution, as it is not designed for long-term use.

Here is a step-by-step guide on how to build a shelter using a poncho:

1. Find a flat, open area to build your shelter. Look for a spot that is protected from the wind and has a solid surface to anchor the poncho to.
2. Lay the poncho out on the ground, with the hood facing up.
3. Use branches, poles, or other long, sturdy objects to create a frame for your shelter. Place them in a teepee shape over the poncho, making sure they are securely anchored to the ground.
4. Cover the frame with the poncho, tucking the edges under the branches or poles to secure it in place.
5. Use the hood of the poncho to create an opening for your shelter. This will help keep out the wind and provide some privacy.
6. Insulate the floor by spreading leaves, moss, or other soft materials on the ground inside the shelter.
7. Make sure to check your shelter frequently, and make adjustments as needed to keep it secure and functional.

Section 3: Long-term Shelters

- Building a shelter using a tent

Building a shelter using a tent is a great way to protect yourself from the elements while camping or in an emergency situation. Here is a step-by-step guide on how to set up a tent:

1. Find a flat, open area to set up your tent. Look for a spot that is protected from the wind and has a solid surface to anchor the tent to.
2. Lay out the tent on the ground, making sure it is fully opened and stretched out.
3. Assemble the tent poles according to the manufacturer's instructions and insert them into the tent.
4. Stake down the corners of the tent using the stakes that came with it, making sure the tent is secure and taut.

5. If your tent has a rainfly, attach it to the tent according to the manufacturer's instructions.
6. Once the tent is set up, make sure to check for any holes or tears in the tent fabric, and repair them using the included patching kit or duct tape.
7. Insulate the floor by spreading a groundsheet or a tarp before setting up your tent.
8. Keep in mind to bring and use a tent footprint which is a separate piece of fabric to put under the tent to protect the tent floor from wear and tear.
9. Make sure to check your tent frequently, and make adjustments as needed to keep it secure and functional.

Tips:

1. Practice setting up your tent in your backyard or a nearby park before you head out on your camping trip.
2. Always use the guylines to secure the tent to the ground, it will help to prevent the tent from collapsing in case of strong winds.
3. Avoid setting up your tent in a low area, where water may collect during a rainstorm.
4. Bring a repair kit with you, in case of any tear or damage to the tent.

Note: Always follow the manufacturer's instructions when setting up your tent.

- Building a shelter using a lean-to

Building a lean-to shelter is a simple and effective way to protect yourself from the elements in a wilderness setting. A lean-to shelter is a structure that consists of a sloping roof supported by one wall, and it can be made using natural materials or man-made materials such as a tarp. Here is a step-by-step guide on how to build a lean-to shelter using natural materials:

1. Find a suitable location to build your shelter. Look for a spot that is protected from the wind, has a solid surface to anchor the shelter, and

is near a source of water.
2. Gather materials to use for the shelter. You will need long branches or poles, smaller branches or twigs, and leaves, moss, or other natural materials to use as insulation.
3. Create a frame for the shelter by leaning two long branches or poles against a tree or other large object.
4. Secure the frame by tying the branches or poles together at the top and at the base, and by staking them into the ground.
5. Gather smaller branches or twigs and place them on top of the frame, creating a sloping roof.
6. Cover the roof with leaves, moss, or other natural materials to provide insulation and protection from the elements.
7. Insulate the ground by spreading leaves, moss, or other natural materials on the ground inside the shelter.
8. Make sure to check your shelter frequently, and make adjustments as needed to keep it secure and functional.

Tips:

1. Make sure the shelter is well ventilated, to prevent condensation from forming.
2. If you are building a lean-to shelter using a tarp, make sure to tie the tarp securely to the shelter frame, and check it frequently for any tears or damage.
3. Always make sure you have permission to build a shelter if you are on private property.

Note: A lean-to shelter is not suitable for heavy rain or strong winds, and it is best used as a temporary shelter in an emergency situation.

- Building a shelter using a debris hut

A debris hut is a type of shelter that can be built using natural materials found in the wilderness, such as branches, leaves, and moss. Building a debris hut is a great way to protect yourself from the elements in a survival situation. Here is a step-by-step guide on how to build a debris hut:

1. Find a suitable location to build your shelter. Look for a spot that is protected from the wind and rain, has a solid surface to anchor the shelter, and is near a source of water.
2. Gather materials to use for the shelter. You will need long branches or poles, smaller branches or twigs, leaves, moss, or other natural materials to use as insulation.
3. Create the frame for the shelter by leaning two long branches or poles against each other, creating a tripod shape.
4. Secure the frame by tying the branches or poles together at the top and at the base, and by staking them into the ground.
5. Gather smaller branches or twigs and place them on top of the frame, creating a sloping roof.
6. Cover the roof with leaves, moss, or other natural materials to provide insulation and protection from the elements.
7. Insulate the ground by spreading leaves, moss, or other natural materials on the ground inside the shelter.
8. To close the front of the shelter, lean branches or twigs in an "A" shape against the frame, and cover them with leaves, moss, or other natural materials to create a doorway.
9. Make sure to check your shelter frequently, and make adjustments as needed to keep it secure and functional.

Tips:

1. Make sure the shelter is well ventilated, to prevent condensation from forming.
2. Always make sure you have permission to build a shelter if you are on private property.
3. When building a debris hut, always make sure to use environmentally-friendly practices and to not harm any living organism or destroy nature.
4. A debris hut is not suitable for heavy rain or strong winds, and it is best used as a temporary shelter in an emergency situation.

Note: Building a debris hut requires some wilderness survival knowledge and experience, so it's important to be familiar with the materials and the area where you will build your shelter.

Section 4: Urban Shelters

- Building a shelter using a cardboard box

Building a shelter using a cardboard box is a quick and easy way to create a temporary shelter in an emergency situation. Cardboard boxes are readily available and can provide a bit of insulation and protection from the elements. Here is a guide on how to build a shelter using a cardboard box:

1. Gather materials: Collect a large cardboard box, duct tape, scissors, a plastic sheet or tarp, and any other materials you may need to secure the shelter in place.
2. Cut a door and windows: Cut a door on one end of the box, and windows on the sides, using scissors. This will allow for ventilation and light.
3. Insulate the box: Line the inside of the box with a plastic sheet or tarp, to keep the inside dry and to help retain heat.
4. Secure the box: Use duct tape to secure the box in place, and to seal any gaps or holes.
5. Anchor the shelter: Use rocks, branches, or other heavy objects to anchor the shelter in place, to prevent it from being blown away.
6. Make a bed: Use leaves, moss, or other natural materials to make a bed inside the box, to keep you off the cold ground.
7. Make a fire: If it's safe and allowed, you can make a fire outside the shelter, to keep warm and cook food.

Tips:

1. Make sure the shelter is well ventilated, to prevent condensation from forming.
2. Always make sure you have permission to build a shelter if you are on private property.
3. Be aware that a cardboard box shelter is not suitable for heavy rain or

strong winds, and it is best used as a temporary shelter in an emergency situation.
4. It's important to use a cardboard box that is clean and doesn't have any chemicals or toxins that may harm you.

Note: Building a shelter using a cardboard box is a quick and easy solution, but it's not a long-term shelter. It's best used as a temporary shelter in an emergency situation, and it's important to have a plan for a more permanent shelter.

- Building a shelter using a sleeping bag

Building a shelter using a sleeping bag is a great way to protect yourself from the elements in a survival situation. A sleeping bag can provide warmth and insulation, but it is not designed to be used as a standalone shelter. Here is a guide on how to build a shelter using a sleeping bag:

1. Find a suitable location to build your shelter. Look for a spot that is protected from the wind and rain, has a solid surface to anchor the shelter, and is near a source of water.
2. Gather materials to use for the shelter. You will need a sleeping bag, a tarp or plastic sheet, and any other materials you may need to secure the shelter in place.
3. Lay the tarp or plastic sheet on the ground, making sure it is large enough to cover the area where you will be sleeping.
4. Secure the corners of the tarp or plastic sheet to the ground using rocks, branches, or other heavy objects, to prevent it from being blown away.
5. Place the sleeping bag on top of the tarp or plastic sheet, making sure it is fully unzipped.
6. Use branches, twigs or anything you can find to create a frame over the sleeping bag, this will help to retain the heat and keep you protected from the elements.
7. Cover the frame with leaves, moss, or other natural materials to provide insulation and protection from the elements.

8. Make sure the shelter is well ventilated, to prevent condensation from forming, and to be able to get fresh air.

Tips:

1. Always make sure you have permission to build a shelter if you are on private property.
2. When building a shelter with a sleeping bag, always make sure to use environmentally-friendly practices and to not harm any living organism or destroy nature.
3. A shelter built with a sleeping bag is not suitable for heavy rain or strong winds, and it is best used as a temporary shelter in an emergency situation.
4. Make sure the shelter is not too tight, you need to have space to move and to be able to get in and out.

Note: Building a shelter using a sleeping bag requires some wilderness survival knowledge and experience, so it's important to be familiar with the materials and the area where you will build your shelter. Also, It's important to have a proper plan for a more permanent shelter.

- Building a shelter using a trash bag

Building a shelter using a trash bag can be a quick and easy way to create a temporary shelter in an emergency situation. Trash bags are readily available and can provide a bit of insulation and protection from the elements. Here is a guide on how to build a shelter using a trash bag:

1. Gather materials: Collect a large trash bag, string or duct tape, scissors, and any other materials you may need to secure the shelter in place.
2. Cut a hole in the trash bag: Cut a hole at one end of the trash bag, large enough for you to crawl through, using scissors.
3. Create a frame: Use branches, sticks or any other materials you can find to create a frame for the shelter. The frame should be tall enough for you to sit up in and wide enough for you to lay down in.

4. Cover the frame with the trash bag: Draping the trash bag over the frame, making sure it's fully covering the frame and secure it with string or duct tape.
5. Secure the shelter: Use rocks, branches, or other heavy objects to anchor the shelter in place, to prevent it from being blown away.
6. Insulate the shelter: Use leaves, moss, or other natural materials to insulate the shelter, to keep you warm and dry.
7. Make a bed: Use leaves, moss, or other natural materials to make a bed inside the shelter, to keep you off the cold ground.
8. Make a fire: If it's safe and allowed, you can make a fire outside the shelter, to keep warm and cook food.

Tips:

1. Make sure the shelter is well ventilated, to prevent condensation from forming.
2. Always make sure you have permission to build a shelter if you are on private property.
3. Be aware that a trash bag shelter is not suitable for heavy rain or strong winds, and it is best used as a temporary shelter in an emergency situation.
4. It's important to use a trash bag that is clean and doesn't have any chemicals or toxins that may harm you.

Note: Building a shelter using a trash bag is a quick and easy solution, but it's not a long-term shelter. It's best used as a temporary shelter in an emergency situation, and it's important to have a plan for a more permanent shelter.

- **Finding and purifying water**

Access to clean and safe drinking water is essential for survival in any situation. In this chapter, we will cover various techniques for finding and purifying water in different environments and situations.

Section 1: Finding Water

- Identifying sources of water in the wilderness

Identifying sources of water in the wilderness is an important skill to have if you are planning to spend time outdoors or in case of emergency. Here are some ways to identify sources of water in the wilderness:

1. Look for signs of water: Look for signs of water such as mossy rocks, green vegetation, or animal tracks leading to a water source. These can be indications that water is nearby.
2. Follow topography: Look for low-lying areas such as valleys, depressions, and ravines, as these areas are more likely to have water. Also, sources of water are more likely to be found near the base of mountains and hills, rather than on top.
3. Listen for running water: Listen for the sound of running water, such as a stream or river. The sound of running water can be heard from a distance and can help you locate a source of water.
4. Check the weather: After a heavy rain, you can check for temporary streams or pools of water.
5. Look for animals: Animals need water to survive, so they can be a good indicator of a water source. Look for animal tracks, droppings, or other signs of animal activity near a water source.
6. Use a map: Look for natural features on a map such as rivers, lakes, or springs, which can be a good indication of a water source.
7. Dig for water: If you are in a dry area, you may need to dig for water. Look for areas where the ground is damp or where there is a slight depression in the ground. Dig a shallow hole, and you may find water seeping into the hole.
8. Use a water purification system: If you do find water, make sure to purify it before drinking it. You can use a water filter, purification tablets or boil the water.

It is important to note that water sources in the wilderness can be unreliable and may dry up during the summer or in dry seasons. So, it's best to carry a water filter, purification tablets, or a water bottle with you when you're going to be in the wilderness.

Also, when you're in a wilderness, it is important to know the local regulations and laws regarding water collection and use in the area you're visiting.

- Locating water in urban environments

Locating water in an urban environment can be a bit more challenging than finding it in the wilderness, but it is still possible. Here are some ways to locate water in an urban environment:

1. Check for man-made sources of water: Look for fountains, public swimming pools, or water features that may contain water that can be used.
2. Look for public restrooms or buildings: Public restrooms and buildings often have running water that can be used in an emergency.
3. Check for fire hydrants: Fire hydrants are a reliable source of water, but you should only use them in case of emergency and with the permission of the authorities.
4. Check for water mains or pipes: Look for large water mains or pipes that may indicate a nearby source of water.
5. Check for water tanks or cisterns: Many buildings and homes have water tanks or cisterns that collect and store rainwater. These can be a good source of water in an emergency.
6. Check for natural sources of water: Even in urban environments, there may be natural sources of water such as rivers, lakes or streams.
7. Ask for Help: Ask for help from local authorities or the community, they may know of a nearby source of water.

It's important to note that when you're in an urban environment, you should always be aware of the potential for contamination, and make sure to purify the water before drinking it.

When you're looking for water in an urban environment, it is important to know the local regulations and laws regarding water collection and use in the area you're visiting.

- Using a map and compass to locate water sources

Using a map and compass to locate water sources can be an effective way to find water in both urban and wilderness environments. Here's how to use a map and compass to locate water sources:

1. Acquire a map: Obtain a topographical map of the area you will be in. This type of map will show the contours of the land and will help you identify potential water sources.
2. Identify potential water sources: Look for natural features such as rivers, lakes, and springs on the map. These can be good indicators of a water source.
3. Determine your location: Use your compass to determine your current location on the map. This will help you navigate to potential water sources.
4. Determine the direction of travel: Using your compass, determine the direction you need to travel to reach the potential water source.
5. Follow the direction of travel: Keeping your compass in hand, follow the direction of travel to reach the potential water source.
6. Check for water: When you reach the potential water source, check to see if there is actually water present. If not, repeat the process with another potential water source.
7. Mark your location: Once you find a water source, mark its location on the map so you can return to it later if needed.

It's important to note that using a map and compass to locate water sources can be challenging and may require some practice to master. It's always a good idea to have a backup plan in case the water source is not found or dried up.

Additionally, when you're looking for water in an urban or wilderness environment, it is important to know the local regulations and laws regarding water collection and use in the area you're visiting.

- Using natural indicators to locate water sources

Using natural indicators to locate water sources is a traditional and effective way to find water in the wilderness. Here's how to use natural indicators to locate water sources:

1. Look for vegetation: Areas with lush vegetation, such as a dense forest or a green oasis in a desert, are likely to have a nearby water source. Look for trees or plants that are commonly found near water, such as cottonwoods, willows, or cattails.
2. Look for animal tracks and signs: Animals need water to survive, so look for tracks and signs that indicate their presence. Look for animal tracks leading to or from a water source, or look for droppings or scat that may indicate the presence of water.
3. Listen for the sound of running water: Listen for the sound of running water, such as a stream or a river. The sound of running water can often be heard from a distance, especially in a quiet environment.
4. Look for natural depressions: Natural depressions, such as low-lying areas or valleys, can collect rainwater and may contain a water source. Look for natural depressions that are surrounded by lush vegetation or that have a small stream or spring flowing through them.
5. Check for rock outcroppings: Water can collect in rock outcroppings and crevices, especially in the desert. Look for rock outcroppings that have moss or lichen growing on them, as these are indicators of a nearby water source.
6. Look for other signs of water: Look for signs of water such as muddy ground, damp soil, or even dew on the plants.

Using natural indicators to locate water sources requires knowledge of the area, and a keen observation. It's also important to know the local regulations and laws regarding water collection and use in the area you're visiting. It's always a good idea to have a backup plan in case the water source is not found or dried up.

- Using a water filter straw or water filter bottle

Using natural indicators to locate water sources is a traditional and effective way to find water in the wilderness. Here's how to use natural indicators to locate water sources:

1. Look for vegetation: Areas with lush vegetation, such as a dense

forest or a green oasis in a desert, are likely to have a nearby water source. Look for trees or plants that are commonly found near water, such as cottonwoods, willows, or cattails.
2. Look for animal tracks and signs: Animals need water to survive, so look for tracks and signs that indicate their presence. Look for animal tracks leading to or from a water source, or look for droppings or scat that may indicate the presence of water.
3. Listen for the sound of running water: Listen for the sound of running water, such as a stream or a river. The sound of running water can often be heard from a distance, especially in a quiet environment.
4. Look for natural depressions: Natural depressions, such as low-lying areas or valleys, can collect rainwater and may contain a water source. Look for natural depressions that are surrounded by lush vegetation or that have a small stream or spring flowing through them.
5. Check for rock outcroppings: Water can collect in rock outcroppings and crevices, especially in the desert. Look for rock outcroppings that have moss or lichen growing on them, as these are indicators of a nearby water source.
6. Look for other signs of water: Look for signs of water such as muddy ground, damp soil, or even dew on the plants.

Using natural indicators to locate water sources requires knowledge of the area, and a keen observation. It's also important to know the local regulations and laws regarding water collection and use in the area you're visiting. It's always a good idea to have a backup plan in case the water source is not found or dried up.

Section 2: Purifying Water

- Boiling water

Boiling water is a simple and effective method to purify water and make it safe to drink. Here's how to boil water:

1. Locate a water source: Use natural indicators, a map and compass, or other methods to locate a clean water source. Make sure the water

source is not contaminated before boiling it.
2. Gather your equipment: You will need a heat source, a pot or container to hold the water, and a fire starter (if using a fire as a heat source).
3. Heat the water: Place the pot or container on the heat source and add water to it. Bring the water to a rolling boil for at least one minute.
4. Turn off the heat and let the water cool: Once the water reaches a rolling boil, turn off the heat and let the water cool for a few minutes before drinking it.
5. Drink the water: Once cooled, the water is safe to drink.

Boiling water is a reliable method for purifying it, but it requires fuel and a heat source. It is important to know the local regulations and laws regarding water collection and use in the area you're visiting. It's always a good idea to have a backup plan in case you don't have the equipment or the ability to boil water.

Note: If you are in a high altitude area, the boiling point of water is lower than sea level. Therefore, it is recommended to boil the water for 3-5 minutes instead of 1 minute to eliminate any bacteria or viruses

- Using water purification tablets

Water purification tablets are a convenient and easy-to-use method to purify water and make it safe to drink. Here's how to use water purification tablets:

1. Locate a water source: Use natural indicators, a map and compass, or other methods to locate a clean water source. Make sure the water source is not contaminated before using purification tablets.
2. Gather your equipment: You will need water purification tablets and a container to hold the water.
3. Fill the container with water: Carefully pour the water from the source into the container.
4. Add the tablets: Follow the instructions on the package of tablets to determine how many tablets you need to add to the water. Usually, one tablet is added to one liter of water.

5. Wait for the recommended time: Allow the tablets to dissolve and purify the water for the recommended time on the package. This usually ranges from 30 minutes to 4 hours.
6. Drink the water: Once the recommended time has passed, the water is safe to drink.

Water purification tablets are a lightweight, easy and convenient method for purifying water, but they are not 100% effective in removing all contaminants and impurities from water. It is recommended to use them in combination with other purification methods such as boiling or using a water filter straw or bottle.

Additionally, when you're using water purification tablets, it is important to know the local regulations and laws regarding water collection and use in the area you're visiting. It's always a good idea to have a backup plan in case the tablets don't work or are not available.

- Using a water filter or water purification system

A water filter or purification system can be a reliable and effective method to purify water and make it safe to drink. Here's how to use a water filter or purification system:

1. Locate a water source: Use natural indicators, a map and compass, or other methods to locate a clean water source. Make sure the water source is not contaminated before using a filter or purification system.
2. Gather your equipment: You will need a water filter or purification system, a container to hold the water, and a source of power if using an electric filter or purification system.
3. Fill the container with water: Carefully pour the water from the source into the container.
4. Connect the filter or purification system: Follow the manufacturer's instructions to properly connect the filter or purification system to the container.
5. Turn on the filter or purification system: If the system is electric, plug it in or insert batteries if required. If the system is manual, begin

pumping or squeezing the water through the filter or purification system.
6. Wait for the recommended time: Allow the water to filter or purify for the recommended time on the manufacturer's instructions.
7. Drink the water: Once the water has been purified, it is safe to drink.

Water filters and purification systems are a reliable and effective method for purifying water, but they require proper maintenance, replacement of filters and cleaning. They also come in different types, some are designed for backpacking, others for camping, and others for emergency situations. It is important to know the local regulations and laws regarding water collection and use in the area you're visiting. It's always a good idea to have a backup plan in case the filter or purification system doesn't work or is not available.

- Using a solar still

A solar still is a device that uses the sun's energy to purify water and make it safe to drink. Here's how to use a solar still:

1. Locate a water source: Use natural indicators, a map and compass, or other methods to locate a clean water source. Make sure the water source is not contaminated before using a solar still.
2. Gather your equipment: You will need a solar still, a container to hold the water, a clear plastic sheet, and a digging tool (if you don't have a pre-made still).
3. Build the still: If you don't have a pre-made still, dig a hole in the ground. The hole should be about 3 feet wide and 2 feet deep. Place the container in the middle of the hole and cover it with the clear plastic sheet. Secure the edges of the plastic sheet with rocks or dirt so that it forms a dome over the container.
4. Place the still in a sunny location: Place the still in a location that receives direct sunlight throughout the day.
5. Wait for the water to evaporate: Allow the sun to heat the water in the container, causing it to evaporate. As the water vapor rises and hits the plastic sheet, it condenses and runs down the sheet into the

container.
6. Drink the water: Once the water has been purified by the solar still, it is safe to drink.

Solar stills are a convenient and easy-to-use method to purify water and make it safe to drink. They are a good option for wilderness survival, camping, and emergency situations, but they require direct sunlight to work. It is recommended to have a backup plan in case the weather conditions don't allow the use of a solar still. Additionally, when you're using a solar still, it is important to know the local regulations and laws regarding water collection and use in the area you're visiting.

- Using a makeshift filter

A makeshift filter is a simple device that can be used to remove dirt, debris, and other contaminants from water. Here's how to use a makeshift filter:

1. Gather materials: To make a makeshift filter, you will need a container, a coffee filter or a piece of clean cloth, charcoal, sand, and gravel.
2. Prepare the container: Clean the container that you will use to hold the filtered water.
3. Layer the materials: In the container, add a layer of gravel at the bottom, followed by a layer of sand, and then a layer of charcoal.
4. Add a filter: Place the coffee filter or cloth on top of the charcoal. This will act as the final barrier to remove any remaining particles.
5. Pour the water: Slowly pour the dirty water over the filter. The water will pass through the filter, removing dirt and debris.
6. Wait for the water to filter: Allow the water to filter through the layers of gravel, sand, and charcoal. This process can take a few minutes to several hours, depending on the amount of water you're filtering and the quality of the water source.
7. Collect the filtered water: Once the water has been filtered, it should be safe to drink. Collect the filtered water in another clean container.

It's important to note that while a makeshift filter can help to remove dirt and debris, it may not remove all microorganisms or chemical contaminants. Therefore, it is recommended to disinfect the filtered water by boiling or using purification tablets before drinking. Additionally, if you're in an emergency situation, it's always best to have a backup plan in case the filter becomes clogged or the water is too dirty to filter.

Section 3: Storing and Transporting Water

- Selecting the right container for storing and transporting water

When selecting a container for storing and transporting water, there are a few key factors to consider:

1. Material: The container should be made of a safe, non-toxic material that won't leach chemicals into the water. Some safe options include plastic, stainless steel, and glass. Avoid containers made of aluminum or copper, as these can react with acidic water and leach harmful chemicals.
2. Durability: The container should be able to withstand the wear and tear of being transported, such as being dropped or bumped. Look for containers made of high-density polyethylene (HDPE) or food-grade stainless steel, which are known for their durability.
3. Capacity: Consider how much water you will need to store and transport. A smaller container will be easier to carry and take up less space, but you'll need more of them to store the same amount of water as a larger container.
4. Portability: The container should be easy to carry and transport, especially if you plan on hiking or traveling with it. Look for containers with handles or straps that allow you to carry them easily.
5. Easy to clean: Look for a container that is easy to clean, and will not retain any smell or taste, as this will affect the water quality.
6. Water tightness: Look for a container that seals tightly to prevent leaks and spills. Look for screw top or flip-top lids, or containers with a tight-fitting lid that can be sealed with a rubber gasket.
7. UV-resistant: UV-resistant containers are better for storing water for

long periods of time, as they prevent the growth of microorganisms in the water.
8. Temperature resistance: If you plan on storing water in extreme temperatures, look for containers that can withstand extreme heat or cold.

Ultimately, the right container for you will depend on your specific needs and the intended use of the container. It's always best to choose a container that is versatile and durable, and can be used for different purposes.

- Treating water for long-term storage

When storing water for long-term use, it is important to properly treat it to ensure that it remains safe to drink. Here are some steps to take when treating water for long-term storage:

1. Clean and sanitize the container: Before storing water, make sure the container is clean and free of any contaminants. Use a mild soap and hot water to wash the container, and then rinse it thoroughly. Sanitize the container by mixing 1 teaspoon of unscented household bleach with a quart of water, and then pouring the solution into the container. Let it sit for a few minutes, then rinse the container thoroughly with clean water.
2. Filter the water: Use a water filter or purification system to remove any impurities or contaminants from the water. This will help to ensure that the water is safe to drink, even after long-term storage.
3. Add a water stabilizer: To prevent the growth of microorganisms in the water, add a water stabilizer such as chlorine dioxide or hydrogen peroxide. Follow the manufacturer's instructions for the proper dosage.
4. Store in a cool, dark place: Water should be stored in a cool, dark place to prevent the growth of microorganisms and to slow down the natural process of water degradation. Avoid storing water in direct sunlight or in an area with high temperatures.
5. Rotate your water supply: Be sure to rotate your water supply every 6

months and check for any discoloration, odor, or any other changes that may indicate the water is no longer safe to drink.
6. Keep water in opaque containers: Light can degrade water over time, so it is best to store water in opaque containers to protect it from light exposure.
7. Avoid using containers that can leach chemicals: Avoid using containers made of aluminum or copper, as these can react with acidic water and leach harmful chemicals.

By following these steps, you can ensure that your stored water remains safe to drink for a long period of time.

- Transporting water safely

Transporting water safely is important to ensure that the water remains safe to drink. Here are some steps to take when transporting water:

1. Use clean and appropriate containers: Make sure the container used to transport water is clean and free of any contaminants. Use food-grade containers specifically designed for water storage, such as water jugs or plastic containers. Avoid using containers made of aluminum or copper, as these can react with acidic water and leach harmful chemicals.
2. Seal the container properly: Make sure the container is properly sealed to prevent any contamination of the water during transport. Use tight-fitting lids or caps and check for leaks before transporting the water.
3. Keep water cool: Water should be kept cool to slow down the growth of microorganisms and to prevent the natural process of water degradation. Avoid storing water in direct sunlight or in an area with high temperatures.
4. Keep water upright: Water should be transported in an upright position to prevent leaks and spills. If possible, use a water carrier with a handle for easy transport.
5. Keep water away from other items: Keep water away from other

items, such as food, chemicals, or dirty equipment, to prevent contamination.
6. Transport water in a safe and reliable vehicle: Make sure the vehicle you use to transport water is safe and reliable, and that the water is properly secured during transport to prevent spills or leaks.
7. Label the container: Label the container with the date the water was stored and any other relevant information, like the source of the water.

- **Starting a fire**

Starting a Fire
Starting a fire is a crucial survival skill that can be used for a variety of purposes such as cooking food, signaling for help, and keeping warm. In this chapter, we will cover various techniques for starting a fire in different environments and situations.
Section 1: Fire-making Materials

- Types of tinder

Tinder is a material that is used to help start a fire. It is typically dry and easily combustible, and it is used to catch a spark or flame from a fire starter, such as a match or a firesteel. There are many different types of tinder that can be used for fire starting, including:

1. Dry leaves and grass: These are readily available in most environments and can be used as tinder. They are easy to ignite and will help to catch a spark or flame.
2. Wood shavings: These can be made by using a knife or a saw to shave thin strips of wood from a piece of wood. They are easy to ignite and will help to catch a spark or flame.
3. Paper: Any kind of paper can be used as tinder. It can be torn into small pieces, and it's easy to ignite and will help to catch a spark or flame.
4. Cotton balls: Cotton balls can be coated with petroleum jelly or wax

to make them highly combustible. They are lightweight and easy to ignite, making them a good option for backpacking.
5. Char cloth: Char cloth is made by charring a piece of cotton fabric in a low-oxygen environment. It is highly combustible and will catch a spark or flame easily.
6. Dryer lint: This is a great option for tinder because it is easily available and easy to ignite. It can be carried in a small container or plastic bag.
7. Magnesium: Magnesium is a highly combustible metal that can be shaved into small pieces and used as tinder. It can be ignited with a spark from a firesteel.
8. Fungi: Some mushrooms are highly combustible and can be used as tinder. They can be found in most wooded areas.

By having a variety of tinder on hand, you can be prepared for any fire-starting situation. It is also important to note that some tinder materials may not be legal or allowed to use in certain areas, so it is best to check the local regulations and laws.

- Types of kindling

Kindling is a material that is used to help start a fire, it is larger and less combustible than tinder, but still small enough to ignite easily, and is used to help establish and grow the fire. Here are some examples of types of kindling:

1. Twigs and small branches: Twigs and small branches can be gathered from the ground or broken off of larger branches. They are a good option for kindling because they are easy to find and can be broken into smaller pieces as needed.
2. Bark: Bark can be peeled off of trees and used as kindling. It is often dry and can be easily broken into smaller pieces.
3. Dry leaves and grass: These can be bunched together and used as kindling. They are easy to ignite and will help to establish the fire.
4. Pine cones: Pine cones can be used as kindling because the resin in them will help to ignite the fire. They are also easy to find in most

wooded areas.
5. Sawdust: Sawdust can be used as kindling if it is dry. It is often a by-product of woodworking and can be found in wood shops or saw mills.
6. Dry moss: Moss can be found on the ground in most wooded areas, it is highly combustible and can be used as kindling.
7. Paper logs: These can be made by rolling up newspaper and securing it with twine or tape. They are a good option for kindling because they are easy to make and easy to ignite.
8. Wood chunks: These are larger pieces of wood that have been split or cut into smaller pieces. They are a good option for kindling because they are easy to find and can be broken into smaller pieces as needed.

- Types of fuel

Fuel is a material that is used to sustain a fire once it has been started. Here are some examples of types of fuel:

1. Wood: Wood is the most common type of fuel used for fires. It can be found in most wooded areas and can be broken down into different sizes for different uses, from tinder and kindling to larger logs for sustained burning.
2. Charcoal: Charcoal is made by burning wood in a low-oxygen environment. It is a popular fuel for grilling and camping.
3. Coal: Coal is a fossil fuel that is mined from the ground. It is often used as a fuel source for heating and electricity generation.
4. Propane: Propane is a hydrocarbon gas that is stored in tanks. It is a popular fuel for camping stoves, lanterns, and portable heaters.
5. Natural Gas: Natural Gas is a hydrocarbon gas that is piped into homes and buildings for heating and cooking.
6. Diesel: Diesel is a type of fuel that is made from crude oil. It is most commonly used as fuel for cars, trucks, and heavy machinery.
7. Gasoline: Gasoline is a type of fuel that is made from crude oil. It is most commonly used as fuel for cars and small engines.
8. Kerosene: Kerosene is a type of fuel that is made from crude oil. It is

commonly used as a fuel for lamps and heaters.
9. Alcohol: Alcohol, such as ethanol or methanol, can be used as a fuel for stoves and lanterns.
10. Biomass: Biomass is a renewable fuel that is made from organic materials, such as wood, grasses, and agricultural waste.

It's important to note that some fuels may not be legal or allowed to use in certain areas, so it is best to check the local regulations and laws. Also, it's always important to use fuel in a sustainable way and not to harm the environment.

Section 2: Fire-making Techniques

- Using matches or a lighter
-
- Matches:

- Safety matches are the most common type of match and can be used to light a fire, candles, or cigarettes.
- To use a safety match, strike it against the rough surface on the side of the matchbox.
- Hold the match by the head and use it to light your desired material, such as kindling for a fire.
-
- Lighter:
- A lighter is a portable device that uses a flammable liquid or gas to create a flame.
- To use a lighter, simply press down on the button or wheel to release the gas or liquid and ignite the flame.
- Hold the lighter to your kindling, paper, or other tinder and wait for it to catch fire.

It's important to be careful when using matches and lighters to avoid any accidental fires or burns. Keep them out of reach of children and never leave them unattended. When you're done using them, make sure they are properly put out and stored safely.

- Using a fire steel or ferro rod

1. Gather your materials: To use a fire steel or ferro rod, you will need the fire steel or rod itself, a striker (usually included with the fire steel or sold separately), and tinder. Good tinder options include dry grass, bark shavings, or cotton balls coated in petroleum jelly.
2. Position your materials: Place the tinder in a pile or nest on a non-flammable surface, such as dirt or rocks. Hold the fire steel or rod in one hand and the striker in the other.
3. Strike the fire steel or ferro rod: Hold the fire steel or rod at a slight angle and use the striker to scrape it down the length of the rod, creating sparks. These sparks will fall onto the tinder, hopefully igniting it.
4. Blow on the embers: Once the tinder is lit, blow gently on the embers to help the fire grow. You can also add small pieces of kindling or small sticks to the fire to help it grow.
5. Keep your fire safe: Once the fire is established, be sure to keep it a safe distance from any flammable materials and never leave it unattended. Make sure the fire is fully extinguished before you leave the area.

It's important to practice using a fire steel or ferro rod before you are in a survival situation. Practice striking the fire steel or ferro rod in different weather conditions and with different types of tinder and kindling to increase your chances of success.

- Using a magnifying glass

1. Gather materials: To use a magnifying glass to start a fire, you will need a magnifying glass, tinder and a sunny day. Good tinder options include dry grass, bark shavings, or cotton balls coated in petroleum jelly.
2. Position the materials: Place the tinder in a pile or nest on a non-flammable surface, such as dirt or rocks. Hold the magnifying glass in one hand and position it directly above the tinder.
3. Angle the magnifying glass: Angle the magnifying glass so that it is aimed at the sun, and the sun's rays are focused on the tinder. It is

important to angle the lens correctly or the sun's rays will not be focused on the tinder.
4. Wait for ignition: With the sun's rays focused on the tinder, wait for the heat to build up and ignite the tinder. This process can take several minutes, so be patient.
5. Blow on the embers: Once the tinder is lit, blow gently on the embers to help the fire grow. You can also add small pieces of kindling or small sticks to the fire to help it grow.
6. Keep your fire safe: Once the fire is established, be sure to keep it a safe distance from any flammable materials and never leave it unattended. Make sure the fire is fully extinguished before you leave the area.

- Using a battery and steel wool

1. Gather materials: To use a battery and steel wool to start a fire, you will need a 9-volt battery, steel wool (grade 000 or finer), and tinder. Good tinder options include dry grass, bark shavings, or cotton balls coated in petroleum jelly.
2. Prepare the steel wool: Take a small amount of steel wool and stretch it out to create a thin, fluffy layer. Place the steel wool on top of the tinder.
3. Connect the battery: Hold one end of the steel wool against the positive (+) terminal of the battery and the other end against the negative (-) terminal.
4. Ignite the steel wool: The steel wool will begin to spark and ignite.
5. Blow on the embers: Once the steel wool is lit, blow gently on the embers to help the fire grow. You can also add small pieces of kindling or small sticks to the fire to help it grow.
6. Keep your fire safe: Once the fire is established, be sure to keep it a safe distance from any flammable materials and never leave it unattended. Make sure the fire is fully extinguished before you leave the area.

- Using a bow drill

1. Gather materials: To use a bow drill, you will need a bow, a spindle, a hearth board, and a bearing block. The bow should be made of a flexible material such as a branch or a piece of cordage. The spindle should be a straight stick, slightly longer than the width of your hand. The hearth board should be a flat piece of wood, and the bearing block can be a stone, a piece of metal, or a second piece of wood.
2. Make a notch: On the edge of the hearth board, create a V-shaped notch by cutting away a small piece of wood. This is where the spindle will rotate, creating friction and heat.
3. Place the spindle: Place the spindle into the notch, with the bottom of the spindle resting on the hearth board.
4. Hold the bearing block: Hold the bearing block in one hand, and press it firmly against the top of the spindle.
5. Use the bow: Hold the bow in one hand, and place the bowstring around the spindle, above the bearing block.
6. Start drilling: Hold the bow steady and begin to drill by moving the bow back and forth, creating a sawing motion. The spindle will rotate, creating friction and heat.
7. Keep drilling: Keep drilling until smoke begins to rise from the notch. Once you see smoke, gently blow on the embers to help the fire grow. You can also add small pieces of kindling or small sticks to the fire to help it grow.
8. Keep your fire safe: Once the fire is established, be sure to keep it a safe distance from any flammable materials and never leave it unattended. Make sure the fire is fully extinguished before you leave the area.

- Using a hand drill

1. Gather materials: To use a hand drill, you will need a spindle, a hearth board, and a bearing block. The spindle should be a straight stick, slightly longer than the width of your hand. The hearth board should be a flat piece of wood, and the bearing block can be a stone, a piece of metal, or a second piece of wood.
2. Make a notch: On the edge of the hearth board, create a V-shaped

notch by cutting away a small piece of wood. This is where the spindle will rotate, creating friction and heat.
3. Place the spindle: Place the spindle into the notch, with the bottom of the spindle resting on the hearth board.
4. Hold the bearing block: Hold the bearing block in one hand, and press it firmly against the top of the spindle.
5. Start drilling: Hold the spindle steady and begin to drill by moving the bearing block up and down the spindle, creating a sawing motion. The spindle will rotate, creating friction and heat.
6. Keep drilling: Keep drilling until smoke begins to rise from the notch. Once you see smoke, gently blow on the embers to help the fire grow. You can also add small pieces of kindling or small sticks to the fire to help it grow.
7. Keep your fire safe: Once the fire is established, be sure to keep it a safe distance from any flammable materials and never leave it unattended. Make sure the fire is fully extinguished before you leave the area.

- Using a fire plow

To use a fire plow, you will need a flat, level surface on which to work, such as a piece of wood or a flat rock. Place the plow on the surface, with the pointed end facing down. Using your feet, press down on the handle of the plow to force the pointed end into the surface. Then, using a sawing motion, move the plow back and forth to create a groove or furrow in the surface. Repeat this process, working in a straight line, until you have created a fire pit or other desired shape.

Here are some additional tips:

- Make sure you are using a dry and appropriate surface, and that you are using the plow correctly.
- Use a smooth and steady motion when using the plow to create the groove.
- Use a good fire-starting material such as char cloth and a fire starter tool like a fire steel or flint, to start your fire in the groove you have

created.

- Using a fire saw

To use a fire saw, follow these steps:

1. Make sure the saw blade is properly attached to the saw frame and that the blade is sharp.
2. Gather dry, dead wood of a suitable size for the saw blade.
3. Clear a flat, level area on the ground where you will saw the wood.
4. Place the log on the ground and position it so that it is stable and will not roll or shift while you are sawing.
5. Place the saw blade on the log where you want to make the cut, with the teeth facing the direction of the cut.
6. Place one foot on the log and the other foot on the saw frame to hold it steady.
7. Grasp the saw handles with both hands and begin sawing, using a steady, back-and-forth motion.
8. Use your body weight to apply pressure to the saw as you push it through the wood.
9. Stop sawing when the blade has cut through the log.
10. Repeat steps 4-9 to saw additional logs as needed.

Section 3: Fire-making in Different Environments

- Starting a fire in wet or humid conditions

Starting a fire in wet or humid conditions can be challenging, but with the right techniques and materials, it is possible. Here are a few tips to help you get a fire going in these conditions:

1. Gather dry, seasoned wood. Wet or green wood will be difficult to ignite and will produce a lot of smoke. Look for dead, dry branches that are easy to break, and use a knife or saw to shave off thin strips of wood to use as kindling.
2. Use a fire starter. Fire starters such as waterproof matches, a fire steel,

or a magnesium fire starter can be used to ignite your kindling.
3. Create a platform for your fire. Building a fire on a raised platform, such as a bed of rocks or bricks, will help to keep the fire off the wet ground and improve airflow.
4. Use a tarp or other waterproof barrier. Place a tarp or other waterproof barrier under your fire to protect it from the damp ground.
5. Build a lean-to shelter. Use branches or other natural materials to create a lean-to shelter around your fire. This will help to block the wind and keep the fire burning.
6. Use dry leaves or moss as kindling. Dry leaves or moss can be used as kindling to help start your fire.
7. Keep your fire small. In wet conditions, a small fire will be easier to start and maintain than a large one.
8. Keep your fire sheltered from the rain. Try to find a spot where the fire will be sheltered from the rain, such as under a tree or inside a cave.

Remember always to follow the fire safety regulations of your area and to have a way to extinguish the fire properly.

- Starting a fire in cold or snowy conditions

Starting a fire in cold or snowy conditions can be difficult, but with the right techniques and materials, it is possible. Here are a few tips to help you get a fire going in these conditions:

1. Gather dry, seasoned wood. Wet or green wood will be difficult to ignite and will produce a lot of smoke. Look for dead, dry branches that are easy to break, and use a knife or saw to shave off thin strips of wood to use as kindling.
2. Use a fire starter. Fire starters such as waterproof matches, a fire steel, or a magnesium fire starter can be used to ignite your kindling, even if it is covered in snow.

3. Create a platform for your fire. Building a fire on a raised platform, such as a bed of rocks or bricks, will help to keep the fire off the cold ground and improve airflow.
4. Use a windbreak. Create a barrier to block the wind and help to protect your fire from the elements.
5. Use insulation. Place dry leaves, moss, or other natural insulation around your fire to help keep it warm.
6. Keep your fire small. In cold conditions, a small fire will be easier to start and maintain than a large one.
7. Keep your fire sheltered from the snow. Try to find a spot where the fire will be sheltered from the snow, such as under a tree or inside a cave.
8. Use an insulated fire pit. A metal fire pit with a lid can help to keep the fire going in cold conditions by trapping heat inside.
9. Keep your hands and feet warm. Wear gloves, warm socks, and insulated boots to keep your hands and feet warm while you are building and maintaining your fire.

Remember always to follow the fire safety regulations of your area and to have a way to extinguish the fire properly. Also, try to have a plan B, in case it's too difficult to start a fire, like carrying a portable camping stove or having a shelter that can keep you warm.

- Starting a fire in high altitude or high wind conditions

Starting a fire in high altitude or high wind conditions can be challenging, but with the right techniques and materials, it is possible. Here are a few tips to help you get a fire going in these conditions:

1. Gather dry, seasoned wood. Wet or green wood will be difficult to ignite and will produce a lot of smoke. Look for dead, dry branches that are easy to break, and use a knife or saw to shave off thin strips of wood to use as kindling.
2. Use a fire starter. Fire starters such as waterproof matches, a fire steel, or a magnesium fire starter can be used to ignite your kindling, even

in high altitude or windy conditions.
3. Create a platform for your fire. Building a fire on a raised platform, such as a bed of rocks or bricks, will help to keep the fire off the ground and improve airflow.
4. Use a windbreak. Create a barrier to block the wind and help to protect your fire from the elements. Use natural materials like rocks, large logs, or branches to create a windbreak around your fire.
5. Build a fire pit. Dig a small pit and line it with rocks to help contain the fire and protect it from the wind.
6. Keep your fire small. In high wind conditions, a small fire will be easier to start and maintain than a large one.
7. Use a fire pan or fire blanket. An aluminum fire pan or fire blanket can be used to protect the fire from the wind and help to keep it burning.
8. Use a tarp or other waterproof barrier. Place a tarp or other waterproof barrier over your fire to protect it from the wind and rain.
9. Use dry leaves or moss as kindling. Dry leaves or moss can be used as kindling to help start your fire.

Remember always to follow the fire safety regulations of your area and to have a way to extinguish the fire properly. Also, it's important to have a plan B, in case it's too difficult to start a fire, like carrying a portable camping stove or having a shelter that can keep you warm. And make sure to be aware of the altitude sickness, high altitude can cause symptoms such as headache, fatigue, and difficulty breathing.

- Starting a fire in desert conditions

Starting a fire in desert conditions can be challenging due to the dry and hot environment, but with the right techniques and materials, it is possible. Here are a few tips to help you get a fire going in the desert:

1. Gather dry, seasoned wood. Wet or green wood will be difficult to ignite and will produce a lot of smoke. Look for dead, dry branches that are easy to break, and use a knife or saw to shave off thin strips of

wood to use as kindling.
2. Use a fire starter. Fire starters such as waterproof matches, a fire steel, or a magnesium fire starter can be used to ignite your kindling, even in hot and dry conditions.
3. Create a fire pit. Dig a small pit in the ground and line it with rocks to help contain the fire and protect it from the wind.
4. Use a windbreak. Create a barrier to block the wind and help to protect your fire from the elements. Use natural materials like rocks, large logs, or branches to create a windbreak around your fire.
5. Use natural materials as kindling. In desert conditions, it can be difficult to find dry wood or other materials to use as kindling. Look for natural materials such as dry grass, leaves, or cactus to help start your fire.
6. Keep your fire small. In hot and dry conditions, a small fire will be easier to start and maintain than a large one.
7. Use a fire pan or fire blanket. An aluminum fire pan or fire blanket can be used to protect the fire from the wind and help to keep it burning.
8. Use a tarp or other waterproof barrier. Place a tarp or other waterproof barrier over your fire to protect it from the wind and rain.
9. Locate your fire in a sheltered spot. Look for a spot that is sheltered from the wind and sun such as a cave or under a tree.

- **Foraging for food**

Foraging for Food

Foraging for food is an essential survival skill that can help you to sustain yourself in the wilderness or other survival situations. In this chapter, we will cover various techniques for finding and procuring food in different environments and situations.

Section 1: Identifying Edible Plants

- Recognizing common wild plants that are safe to eat

Recognizing common wild plants that are safe to eat can be difficult, as many plants have toxic look-alikes. It's important to be sure of the plant's identity before consuming it. Here are a few tips to help you recognize common wild plants that are safe to eat:

1. Learn the basic characteristics of safe plants. Familiarize yourself with the characteristics of common wild plants that are safe to eat such as leaves, flowers, fruits, and seeds.
2. Learn about the plants that are native to your area. Research the plants that are native to your area, and learn to identify them by their leaves, flowers, fruits, and seeds.
3. Use a field guide. Carry a field guide with you when you are out in the wild, and use it to identify plants.
4. Learn to recognize poisonous plants. Familiarize yourself with the characteristics of plants that are poisonous, so that you can avoid them.
5. Learn from an expert. Take a class or workshop with an expert in wild plant identification, or go on a guided hike with a naturalist.
6. Start small and easy. Start by learning to identify a few easy-to-identify, common and safe wild plants such as dandelions, wild strawberries, and blackberries.
7. Don't eat a wild plant if you are not sure about it. If you are not sure about the identity of a plant, don't eat it. It's better to be safe than sorry.
8. Double check before consuming. Even if you're certain that you've correctly identified a plant, it's a good idea to double-check with a field guide or expert before consuming it.

- Differentiating between poisonous and non-poisonous plants

Differentiating between poisonous and non-poisonous plants can be difficult, as many plants have toxic look-alikes. It's important to be sure of the plant's identity before consuming it. Here are a few tips to help you differentiate between poisonous and non-poisonous plants:

1. Learn the basic characteristics of poisonous plants. Familiarize yourself with the characteristics of poisonous plants, such as leaves, flowers, fruits, and seeds. Some common indicators of a poisonous plant include a milky or discolored sap, a bitter or soapy taste, a pungent or acrid smell, or a shiny or waxy surface on the leaves.
2. Learn about the poisonous plants that are native to your area. Research the poisonous plants that are native to your area, and learn to identify them by their leaves, flowers, fruits, and seeds.
3. Use a field guide. Carry a field guide with you when you are out in the wild, and use it to identify plants, many field guides have sections specifically dedicated to poisonous plants.
4. Learn from an expert. Take a class or workshop with an expert in wild plant identification, or go on a guided hike with a naturalist, experts can give you more detailed information and help you learn about the poisonous plants of your area.
5. Pay attention to the plant's environment. Some poisonous plants will only be found in certain environments such as wetlands or in the forest, and this can be a good indicator of a poisonous plant.
6. Don't eat a wild plant if you are not sure about it. If you are not sure about the identity of a plant, don't eat it. It's better to be safe than sorry.
7. Learn the symptoms of poisoning. Familiarize yourself with the symptoms of poisoning, so that you can quickly recognize them if you come into contact with a poisonous plant.
8. Don't rely on folklore or traditional uses. Just because a plant has been used traditionally does not mean that it is safe to eat, always be sure to properly identify the plant before consuming it.

- Using a field guide or plant identification app

A field guide or plant identification app can be a valuable tool for identifying wild plants. Here are a few tips on how to use them:

1. Familiarize yourself with the layout of the field guide or app. Understand where to find information on the plant's characteristics,

such as leaves, flowers, fruits, and seeds.
2. Use the index or search feature to find the plant you're looking for. Many field guides and apps have a built-in index or search feature that allows you to quickly find the plant you're looking for.
3. Look for physical characteristics. Compare the plant you've found to the pictures and descriptions in the field guide or app to find a match. Pay attention to details such as leaf shape, flower color, and fruit characteristics.
4. Use the range maps. Many field guides and apps include range maps that show where a plant is typically found, which can help narrow down the possibilities.
5. Compare multiple sources. When using a field guide or app, compare the information from multiple sources to verify the identification of the plant.
6. Be aware of the limitations of the field guide or app. Not all field guides or apps include every plant species, and some may not be as detailed as others, so it's important to be aware of the limitations of your field guide or app.
7. Take a picture and use the apps identification feature. Many plant identification apps have feature that allows you to take a picture of the plant, which will then be used by the app to identify the plant.
8. Always double-check. Even if you're certain that you've correctly identified a plant with the help of field guide or app, it's a good idea to double-check with an expert or another source before consuming it.

By following these tips, you can increase your chances of correctly identifying wild plants. However, always be cautious when consuming wild plants, and if you are uncertain about their safety, it's best to not eat them. And always be aware of the laws and regulations of your area, some plants are protected or prohibited in some areas.

Section 2: Foraging Techniques

- Collecting wild berries and fruits

Collecting wild berries and fruits can be a fun and rewarding experience, but it's important to do it safely and responsibly. Here are a few tips on how to collect wild berries and fruits:

1. Learn to identify the plants. Before collecting wild berries or fruits, learn to identify the plants and make sure they are safe to eat. Research the poisonous plants that are native to your area, and learn to identify them by their leaves, flowers, fruits, and seeds.
2. Know the regulations. Be aware of any laws and regulations regarding the collection of wild berries and fruits in your area. Some plants are protected or prohibited in certain areas, and it's important to know what you can and can't collect.
3. Only collect from areas that are free from pollution. Avoid collecting wild berries or fruits from areas that are close to roads, industrial sites, or other sources of pollution.
4. Be mindful of the time of year. Different berries and fruits ripen at different times of the year, so be sure to collect them at the right time for the best flavor and quality.
5. Use proper tools. Use tools such as gloves and a small basket or container to collect wild berries or fruits. This will help keep the berries or fruits from getting crushed and make it easier to transport them.
6. Be respectful of the environment. When collecting wild berries or fruits, be mindful of the environment and avoid damaging the plants or the surrounding ecosystem.
7. Only collect what you need. Collect only what you need for your immediate use and never take more than you can use.
8. Leave some for wildlife. Remember that wild berries and fruits are an important food source for wildlife, so always leave some behind for them to enjoy.

By following these tips, you can safely and responsibly collect wild berries and fruits while preserving the environment for future generations.

Remember, always be cautious when consuming wild plants, and if you are uncertain about their safety, it's best to not eat them. And always be aware of the laws and regulations of your area, some plants are protected or prohibited in some areas.

- Collecting nuts and seeds

Collecting nuts and seeds can be a fun and rewarding experience, but it's important to do it safely and responsibly. Here are a few tips on how to collect nuts and seeds:

1. Learn to identify the plants. Before collecting nuts and seeds, learn to identify the plants and make sure they are safe to eat. Research the poisonous plants that are native to your area, and learn to identify them by their leaves, flowers, fruits, and seeds.
2. Know the regulations. Be aware of any laws and regulations regarding the collection of nuts and seeds in your area. Some plants are protected or prohibited in certain areas, and it's important to know what you can and can't collect.
3. Only collect from areas that are free from pollution. Avoid collecting nuts and seeds from areas that are close to roads, industrial sites, or other sources of pollution.
4. Be mindful of the time of year. Different nuts and seeds ripen at different times of the year, so be sure to collect them at the right time for the best flavor and quality.
5. Use proper tools. Use tools such as gloves and a small basket or container to collect nuts and seeds. This will help keep the nuts and seeds from getting crushed and make it easier to transport them.
6. Be respectful of the environment. When collecting nuts and seeds, be mindful of the environment and avoid damaging the plants or the surrounding ecosystem.
7. Only collect what you need. Collect only what you need for your immediate use and never take more than you can use.
8. Leave some for wildlife. Remember that nuts and seeds are an important food source for wildlife, so always leave some behind for them to enjoy.
9. Dry and store the nuts properly. Before storing the nuts, make sure to

dry them properly. Store them in an airtight container in a cool, dry place away from direct sunlight.

- Digging for roots and tubers

Digging for roots and tubers can be a great way to gather wild food, but it's important to do it safely and responsibly. Here are a few tips on how to dig for roots and tubers:

1. Learn to identify the plants. Before digging for roots and tubers, learn to identify the plants and make sure they are safe to eat. Research the poisonous plants that are native to your area, and learn to identify them by their leaves, flowers, fruits, and roots.
2. Know the regulations. Be aware of any laws and regulations regarding the collection of roots and tubers in your area. Some plants are protected or prohibited in certain areas, and it's important to know what you can and can't collect.
3. Only dig from areas that are free from pollution. Avoid digging for roots and tubers from areas that are close to roads, industrial sites, or other sources of pollution.
4. Be mindful of the time of year. Different roots and tubers ripen at different times of the year, so be sure to dig them up at the right time for the best flavor and quality.
5. Use proper tools. Use tools such as gloves and a small shovel or trowel to dig for roots and tubers. This will help you to dig up the roots and tubers without damaging the surrounding plants and soil.
6. Be respectful of the environment. When digging for roots and tubers, be mindful of the environment and avoid damaging the plants or the surrounding ecosystem.
7. Only dig what you need. Dig only what you need for your immediate use and never take more than you can use.
8. Leave some for wildlife. Remember that roots and tubers are an important food source for wildlife, so always leave some behind for them to enjoy.
9. Clean and prepare the roots and tubers properly. Before eating, make

sure to clean and prepare the roots and tubers properly. Some roots and tubers need to be cooked before eating, and some may need to be peeled, or soaked in water to remove any toxins.

- Hunting and trapping small game

Hunting and trapping small game can be a great way to gather food in the wild, but it's important to do it safely and responsibly. Here are a few tips on how to hunt and trap small game:

1. Learn the regulations. Before hunting or trapping small game, be familiar with the laws and regulations in your area. Make sure you have the proper licenses and permits, and be aware of the hunting and trapping seasons for the animals you plan to hunt or trap.
2. Learn to identify the animals. Learn to identify the animals you plan to hunt or trap, and understand their habits and habitats. This will help you to locate them more easily and increase your chances of success.
3. Use the appropriate gear. Use the proper gear for hunting or trapping small game, such as a hunting rifle or bow, or a trap. Make sure your gear is in good working condition and that you are familiar with how to use it.
4. Practice ethical hunting and trapping. Always follow ethical hunting and trapping practices, such as using humane traps and ensuring a quick and humane kill.
5. Be mindful of the environment. When hunting or trapping small game, be mindful of the environment and avoid damaging the surrounding ecosystem.
6. Only take what you need. Only take the number of animals that you need for your immediate use, and never take more than you can use.
7. Respect the animals. Remember that animals are living beings and should be respected.
8. Respect other hunters and trappers. Be aware of other hunters and trappers in the area and avoid interfering with their activities.
9. Know how to process the animal. It's important to know how to

properly process the animal after it's been hunted or trapped. This includes cleaning, skinning, and butchering the animal to make it safe for consumption.
10. Learn survival skills. Make sure you have the necessary survival skills to survive in the wilderness, such as building a shelter, finding water, and making fire.

- Fishing

Fishing is a popular pastime that can provide a source of food and recreation. Here are a few basic steps on how to fish:

1. Obtain a fishing license. Before you start fishing, make sure you have the proper licenses and permits for the area you plan to fish in.
2. Choose the right equipment. The type of fishing you plan to do will determine the equipment you need. For example, for freshwater fishing, you will typically need a fishing rod and reel, hooks, lures or bait, and a fishing line. For saltwater fishing, you may also need a fishing rod and reel, but you will also need heavier tackle and different types of bait.
3. Learn about the fish you're trying to catch. Familiarize yourself with the types of fish you plan to catch, their habits and habitats, and the best times and places to catch them.
4. Choose the right bait. Different types of fish are attracted to different types of bait. Some common baits for freshwater fishing include worms, minnows, and artificial lures. Saltwater fishing typically requires live or frozen bait such as squid, or cut bait.
5. Find a good spot to fish. Look for areas where fish are likely to congregate, such as near drop-offs, logs, or other structure.
6. Cast your line. Hold the fishing rod with both hands, and use your dominant hand to hold the reel. Hold the line with your other hand, and use a smooth, sweeping motion to cast the line out into the water.
7. Wait for a bite. Once your line is in the water, wait patiently for a fish to bite. Keep an eye on the line or the fishing rod tip to detect when a fish takes the bait.

8. Set the hook. When you feel a fish biting, quickly set the hook by pulling back on the fishing rod. This will ensure that the fish is securely hooked and won't be able to escape.
9. Reel in the fish. Once the fish is hooked, begin reeling it in by turning the reel handle with your dominant hand. Keep the fishing rod tip up to keep the line tight, and use your other hand to guide the fish in.
10. Release or Keep the fish. If you are keeping the fish you caught, make sure to properly clean and prepare it for cooking or storing. If you decide to release the fish, handle it carefully and release it back into the water as soon as possible to minimize stress.

Fishing can be a fun and rewarding experience, but it's important to follow all local laws and regulations, as well as fishing ethics to make sure you're not overfishing or damaging the ecosystem in any way. Additionally, it's important to be aware of the specific species you are trying to catch, and their specific conservation status, and make sure you're not breaking any regulations.

- Building snares and traps

Section 3: Foraging in Different Environments

- Foraging in the desert

Building snares and traps can be an effective way to catch small game for survival or hunting. Here are a few basic steps on how to build snares and traps:

1. Choose the right location. Look for areas where small game is likely to travel, such as game trails, water sources, or food sources.
2. Gather materials. You will need materials such as wire or cordage to make the snare or trap, as well as natural materials such as twigs, branches, or leaves to camouflage the trap.
3. Make the snare. A snare is a simple device that uses a noose to catch an animal. To make a snare, tie a loop of wire or cordage to a stick or branch, and place the noose over a game trail or other area where an animal is likely to pass through.
4. Make the trap. A trap is a more complex device that uses a trigger

mechanism to catch an animal. To make a trap, you will need to construct a frame using sticks or branches, and then attach a trigger mechanism, such as a bent stick, to the frame. Once the animal trips the trigger, the trap will close and capture the animal.
5. Set the snare or trap. Once your snare or trap is complete, set it in the desired location and camouflage it with natural materials to make it less visible to the animal.
6. Check the snare or trap regularly. Make sure to check your snare or trap regularly to check if an animal is caught and to prevent injury to the animal.
7. Release or Keep the animal. If you are keeping the animal you caught, make sure to properly clean and prepare it for cooking or storing. If you decide to release the animal, handle it carefully and release it back into the wild as soon as possible to minimize stress.

- Foraging in the jungle

Foraging for food in the desert can be challenging due to the harsh conditions and limited resources. However, with the right knowledge and skills, it is possible to find edible plants and other sources of food in the desert. Here are a few tips on how to forage in the desert:

1. Learn to identify edible plants. Familiarize yourself with the common desert plants that are safe to eat, such as cacti, mesquite beans, and yucca. There are also field guides and plant identification apps that can help you identify these plants.
2. Look for sources of water. In the desert, finding water is essential for survival. Look for signs of water, such as dry riverbeds, rock pools, or areas where vegetation is denser than the surrounding area.
3. Look for animal tracks. Animals need water to survive, so following their tracks can lead you to a source of water.
4. Hunt for small game. Desert animals such as lizards, snakes, and small rodents can provide a source of protein.
5. Look for insects. Some insects, such as beetles and caterpillars, can be a source of food in the desert.

6. Be aware of the time of day. Some desert plants are only edible at certain times of the day or in certain seasons, so be aware of when to collect them.
7. Know the laws and regulations. In some areas, hunting and foraging may be illegal or regulated, so be sure to check the laws and regulations before foraging.

- Foraging in the arctic

Foraging for food in the Arctic can be difficult due to the harsh and remote conditions. However, with the right knowledge and skills, it is possible to find food in the Arctic. Here are a few tips on how to forage in the Arctic:

1. Learn to identify edible plants. Familiarize yourself with the common Arctic plants that are safe to eat, such as berries, mosses, and lichens.
2. Look for sources of protein. Arctic animals such as caribou, musk oxen, and fish can provide a source of protein. Hunting and fishing in the Arctic requires specialized equipment and training, so it is important to be familiar with the laws and regulations before attempting to hunt or fish.
3. Look for animal tracks. Following animal tracks can lead you to a source of food.
4. Look for bird eggs. Some Arctic birds, such as geese, lay eggs that are safe to eat.
5. Look for insects. Some insects, such as beetles and caterpillars, can be a source of food in the Arctic.
6. Be aware of the weather. The Arctic weather can change rapidly and unexpectedly, so it's important to be prepared for extreme cold, wind, and snow.
7. Know the laws and regulations. In some areas, hunting and foraging may be illegal or regulated, so be sure to check the laws and regulations before foraging.

- Foraging in urban environments

Foraging for food in urban environments can be a unique and sustainable way to find fresh, healthy food. Here are a few tips on how to forage in urban environments:

1. Learn to identify edible plants. Familiarize yourself with the common urban plants that are safe to eat, such as fruit trees, berry bushes, and herbs.
2. Look for community gardens. Many cities have community gardens where residents can grow their own food. These gardens may be open to the public, or require a membership.
3. Look for farmer's markets. Many cities have farmer's markets where you can buy fresh, locally grown produce.
4. Look for wild edibles. Some urban areas have wild edibles such as dandelions, clover, and purslane.
5. Look for abandoned fruit trees. Some urban areas have abandoned fruit trees that may still bear fruit.
6. Be aware of the laws and regulations. In some cities, foraging may be illegal or regulated, so be sure to check the laws and regulations before foraging.
7. Learn about urban foraging safety. It's important to be aware of the potential risks of foraging in urban environments, such as pollution and pesticides, and take necessary precautions.

It's important to note that foraging for food in urban environments can be a great way to find fresh, healthy food, but it's essential to be knowledgeable about plants identification and safety. Additionally, it's important to be aware of the specific area you are foraging and make sure you're not breaking any regulations and respecting the private property rights.

- **Navigation and orienteering**

Navigation and Orienteering

Navigation and orienteering are essential survival skills that can help you to find your way in the wilderness or other survival situations. In this chapter, we will cover various techniques for navigating and orienteering in different environments and situations.

Section 1: Basic Navigation Techniques

- Using a map and compass

Using a map and compass is a valuable skill for navigating in wilderness and unfamiliar areas. Here are some steps on how to use a map and compass:

1. Familiarize yourself with your map. Before you set out, study the map to get a sense of the terrain, landmarks, and trails. Look for features such as hills, valleys, rivers, and roads.
2. Learn how to read a map. Understand the different symbols and colors used on the map to indicate different types of terrain and features.
3. Learn how to use a compass. A compass is a tool that helps you determine direction. It has a rotating magnetic needle that points to magnetic north.
4. Hold the compass level, and point the direction of travel arrow on the base plate at the destination on the map.
5. Rotate the housing of the compass so that the red end of the needle is pointing to the orienting arrow.
6. Line up the edge of the base plate with the corresponding edge of the map. The direction of travel arrow will now point towards your destination.
7. Take a bearing. A bearing is a measurement of the direction you are facing relative to magnetic north. To take a bearing, point the direction of travel arrow on the base plate at a landmark on the map, and rotate the housing of the compass so that the red end of the needle is pointing to the orienting arrow. The number at the index line is the bearing.
8. Follow your bearing. Once you've taken a bearing, use it to navigate towards your destination. Keep an eye out for landmarks and features that match the map, and adjust your bearing as necessary.
9. Check your position regularly. Use your map and compass to check

your position frequently, and adjust your course if necessary.

- Using a GPS device

Using a GPS (Global Positioning System) device can be a helpful tool for navigation, both in the wilderness and in urban areas. Here are some steps on how to use a GPS device:

1. Turn on the device and wait for it to acquire a signal. This can take a few minutes, and the device may need to be in an open area to receive a signal.
2. Enter your destination. Most GPS devices allow you to enter a destination by address, coordinates, or point of interest.
3. Set the device to navigate to your destination. Once you have entered your destination, the device will calculate the best route and provide turn-by-turn directions.
4. Follow the device's instructions. As you move, the device will provide updates on your location and the distance to your destination, as well as turn-by-turn directions.
5. Keep an eye on the map. The device will display a map showing your current location, your destination, and your route. This can be useful for orienting yourself and for checking your progress.
6. Use the device's other features. Many GPS devices have additional features, such as the ability to track your route and save it for later, mark waypoints, and search for nearby points of interest.
7. Be aware of the device's limitations. GPS devices rely on a signal from satellites, so they may not work in all areas or under certain conditions. For example, they may not work in deep canyons, thick forests or underground. Additionally, they may not provide real-time traffic updates or other information.
8. Keep extra batteries or power bank with you, as some GPS devices can use up a lot of battery power, especially with constant use of the screen.

It's important to note that a GPS device is a helpful tool for navigation, but you should always be aware of the specific area you are navigating in, and take into account the specific conditions such as weather, light, and terrain. Additionally, it's important to practice using a GPS device before setting out on a trip, and to be aware of the specific laws and regulations regarding navigation in the area you are visiting.

- Using natural landmarks and features

Using natural landmarks and features for navigation can be a helpful way to orient yourself and stay on course when you are in the wilderness. Here are some steps on how to use natural landmarks and features for navigation:

1. Learn to recognize common natural landmarks and features. Before you set out on a trip, it's a good idea to familiarize yourself with the types of natural landmarks and features you are likely to encounter in the area. Some examples include mountains, rivers, lakes, and valleys.
2. Take note of these landmarks and features as you travel. As you move through the wilderness, take note of the natural landmarks and features around you. This will help you to orient yourself and stay on course.
3. Use a map and compass to match the natural landmarks and features with your location on the map. If you have a map and compass, use them to match the natural landmarks and features you see with your location on the map. This will help you to know where you are and where you are going.
4. Use the sun and stars to navigate. The sun and stars can be used to navigate in the wilderness as well. You can use the position of the sun to determine your direction and the time of day, and at night you can use the North Star to determine your direction.
5. Pay attention to the landscape. The terrain, vegetation and animal tracks can give you clues about where you are and where to go.
6. Keep a journal. Keeping a journal of the natural landmarks and features you encounter can help you to remember the route you took and make it easier to retrace your steps if necessary.

- Using the sun, stars, and moon

Using the sun, stars, and moon can be a helpful way to navigate in the wilderness. Here are some steps on how to use the sun, stars, and moon for navigation:

1. Learn to recognize the major constellations. Before you set out on a trip, it's a good idea to familiarize yourself with the major constellations in the night sky. Some examples include the Big Dipper, Orion, and the North Star.
2. Use the sun to determine direction during the day. The sun rises in the east and sets in the west, so you can use the sun to determine east and west. In the morning, the sun will be in the east, and in the evening, it will be in the west.
3. Use the North Star to determine direction at night. The North Star, also known as Polaris, is located close to the North Celestial Pole and is a steady point in the night sky. It is a useful reference point for determining direction at night.
4. Use the moon to determine direction. The moon moves across the sky from east to west, and its phase can indicate the time of the month. A crescent moon, for example, can indicate that the moon is in the first or last quarter of the lunar month.
5. Use a compass to confirm your direction. Even if you are using the sun, stars, and moon to navigate, it's always a good idea to use a compass as a backup.

It's important to note that using the sun, stars, and moon for navigation can be challenging and requires practice and knowledge. It's a good idea to learn from experienced hikers or wilderness survival experts, and to practice using the sun, stars, and moon before setting out on a trip. Additionally, it's important to be aware of the specific laws and regulations regarding navigation in the area you are visiting.

Section 2: Orienteering Techniques

- Taking a bearing

Taking a bearing refers to determining the direction of a specific point or location using a compass. Here are the steps to take a bearing:

1. Hold the compass level and steady in your hand. Make sure the compass is away from metal objects and electronic devices, which can interfere with the compass's accuracy.
2. Locate the desired point or location you want to determine the direction for. This could be a specific landmark, a point on a map, or a destination you want to reach.
3. Rotate the bezel, or outer ring of the compass, so that the compass's north arrow lines up with the north arrow on the baseplate.
4. Hold the compass in front of you, with the direction of travel arrow pointing towards the point or location you want to determine the direction for.
5. Turn your body until the red end of the needle is lined up with the north arrow on the baseplate. The bearing, or direction, is the angle between the direction of travel arrow and the north arrow on the baseplate.
6. Record the bearing. It's a good idea to write down the bearing and note the time and location in case you need to refer to it later.
7. To follow the bearing, align the direction of travel arrow with the bearing you have taken and walk in that direction. Remember to keep an eye on your surroundings and adjust your bearing as necessary.

- Using a pace count

A pace count is a method of measuring distance traveled by counting the number of steps taken. Here's how to use a pace count:

1. Determine your pace count by walking a known distance, such as 100 meters, and counting the number of steps it takes you to cover that distance. This is your pace count.
2. Start counting your steps as you begin walking.
3. Every time you reach a certain number of steps, mark the distance you have traveled by using a stick, rock or other visible marker.

4. Continue counting your steps and marking the distance until you reach your destination.
5. To calculate the distance you have traveled, multiply the number of pace counts by the length of your pace. For example, if your pace count is 50 steps per 100 meters, and you have taken 100 pace counts, you have traveled 5000 meters.
6. Keep in mind that your pace count may change based on the terrain, your level of fatigue, and the weight of your pack. Be sure to recalculate your pace count as needed.

- Measuring distance on a map

Measuring distance on a map is a useful skill for navigation and trip planning. Here's how to do it:

1. Obtain a map of the area you will be traveling in. Make sure the map is scaled correctly and has a legend or key that shows the scale of the map.
2. Locate the starting point and the end point on the map.
3. Measure the distance between the two points using a ruler or a measuring tool specifically designed for maps (such as a map measurer).
4. Compare the distance on the map to the scale of the map. The scale is usually located in the legend or key of the map and it will tell you how many kilometers or miles one millimeter or centimeter represents on the map.
5. If the scale of the map is in kilometers, you can convert the distance to miles using a conversion factor of 1.6 kilometers per mile.
6. Note that the distance measured on the map will be the straight-line distance between the two points, not the actual distance you will have to travel on the ground. Remember that the actual distance will be longer due to terrain, obstacles and other factors.
7. If you want to calculate the distance along a certain route, you could use a protractor to measure the angle of the route, and then use trigonometry to calculate the distance.

- Triangulation

Triangulation is a method of determining one's position by measuring angles to two or more known points. Here's how to use triangulation for navigation:

1. Identify two or more visible landmarks that you can use as reference points. These landmarks could be natural features such as mountain peaks or man-made features such as radio towers or buildings.
2. Measure the angle between each landmark and your current position using a compass or an inclinometer.
3. Plot the reference points and the angles on a map of the area.
4. Draw lines from each reference point to the position where the angle was measured.
5. The point where the lines intersect is your current position.
6. Repeat the process with different landmarks to confirm your position.
7. Keep in mind that accurate measurement of angles is essential for accurate triangulation.

- Resection

Resection is a method of determining one's position by measuring angles to two or more known points and a map. Here's how to use resection for navigation:

1. Identify two or more visible landmarks that you can use as reference points. These landmarks could be natural features such as mountain peaks or man-made features such as radio towers or buildings.
2. Measure the angle between each landmark and your current position using a compass or an inclinometer.
3. Plot the reference points and the angles on a map of the area.
4. Draw lines from each reference point to the position where the angle was measured.
5. Use the map to measure the angles between the reference points and the position where the angle was measured.

6. Compare the measured angles to the angles on the map. The point where the angles match is your current position.
7. Repeat the process with different landmarks to confirm your position.

- Back bearing

Back bearing refers to the process of determining the direction from which a line or bearing originates. It is typically used in navigation, surveying, and other fields that involve determining direction and location. To determine the back bearing, one typically measures the angle between the line or bearing and true north, and then adds or subtracts 180 degrees, depending on the context and conventions used.

Section 3: Navigation and Orienteering in Different Environments

- Navigation and orienteering in the desert

Navigating in the desert can be challenging due to the lack of landmarks and the potential for extreme heat and dehydration. However, with proper planning and preparation, it is possible to safely navigate and orient yourself in this type of environment.

1. Plan ahead: Before embarking on a desert adventure, it is important to research the area and plan your route. Take into account factors such as water sources, potential hazards, and the time of day. Make sure to have a detailed map and compass, and consider bringing a GPS device as a backup.
2. Stay hydrated: The heat in the desert can be intense and can quickly dehydrate you. Make sure to bring enough water and to drink it regularly, even if you don't feel thirsty. Additionally, try to avoid strenuous activity during the hottest part of the day.
3. Use the sun and stars: The sun and stars can be used as natural markers to navigate. In the morning, use the rising sun to determine east and west, and in the evening, use the setting sun to determine west and east. During the night, use the North Star to determine

north.
4. **Look for landmarks:** The desert may seem barren and featureless, but keep an eye out for natural landmarks such as rock formations, dunes, and valleys. These can be used to help orient yourself and to confirm your location.
5. **Stay on track:** It can be easy to lose your way in the desert, particularly when visibility is low. Use your map, compass, and landmarks to stay on track and to avoid getting lost. If you do become disoriented, stop and take a moment to reorient yourself before continuing.
6. **Be prepared for emergency:** The desert environment can be harsh and unforgiving, so it is important to be prepared for an emergency. Make sure to bring a first-aid kit, a signal whistle, a flashlight, and other essentials. Also, let someone know your plan and when to expect you back.
7. **Be respectful of the environment:** Remember that the desert is a fragile ecosystem, and it's essential to minimize your impact on the environment. Stick to established trails and campsites, and don't leave any trash behind.

By following these tips, you can navigate and orient yourself safely in the desert. Remember to be prepared and to take the necessary precautions to stay safe, hydrated, and on track.

- Navigation and orienteering in the jungle

Navigating in the jungle can be challenging due to the thick vegetation, varied terrain, and potential for poor visibility. However, with proper planning and preparation, it is possible to safely navigate and orient yourself in this type of environment.

1. **Plan ahead:** Before embarking on a jungle adventure, it is important to research the area and plan your route. Take into account factors such as potential hazards, water sources, and the time of day. Make sure to have a detailed map and compass, and consider bringing a

GPS device as a backup.
2. Stay on a trail: The jungle can be dense and difficult to navigate, so it's essential to stay on established trails whenever possible. These trails will typically offer the easiest and safest passage through the jungle and will also help minimize your impact on the environment.
3. Use the sun and stars: The sun and stars can be used as natural markers to navigate. In the morning, use the rising sun to determine east and west, and in the evening, use the setting sun to determine west and east. During the night, use the North Star to determine north.
4. Look for landmarks: The jungle may seem dense and featureless, but keep an eye out for natural landmarks such as rivers, large trees, and rock formations. These can be used to help orient yourself and to confirm your location.
5. Be aware of the wildlife: The jungle is home to a wide variety of wildlife, some of which can be dangerous. Be aware of your surroundings and the potential for encounters with animals such as snakes, crocodiles, and big cats.
6. Be prepared for emergency: The jungle environment can be harsh and unforgiving, so it is important to be prepared for an emergency. Make sure to bring a first-aid kit, a signal whistle, a flashlight, and other essentials. Also, let someone know your plan and when to expect you back.
7. Be respectful of the environment: Remember that the jungle is a fragile ecosystem, and it's essential to minimize your impact on the environment. Stick to established trails and campsites, and don't leave any trash behind.
8. Follow the right signs: Many Jungle trails are marked with signs such as ribbons, markers, and paint. Follow these signs to stay on track, and avoid getting lost in the jungle.

- Navigation and orienteering in the arctic

Navigating in the Arctic can be challenging due to the extreme cold, limited daylight, and potential for poor visibility. However, with proper planning and preparation, it is possible to safely navigate and orient yourself in this type of environment.

1. Plan ahead: Before embarking on an Arctic adventure, it is important to research the area and plan your route. Take into account factors such as the weather forecast, potential hazards, and the time of day. Make sure to have a detailed map and compass, and consider bringing a GPS device as a backup.
2. Dress for the weather: The Arctic can be extremely cold, so it is essential to dress appropriately. Make sure to wear insulated and waterproof clothing, as well as a hat, gloves, and warm boots.
3. Use the sun and stars: In the Arctic, the sun can only be seen for a few hours a day, so it's essential to use other natural markers to navigate. During the day, use the sun to determine east and west, and during the night, use the stars to determine north.
4. Look for landmarks: The Arctic can be barren and featureless, but keep an eye out for natural landmarks such as mountains, valleys, and ice formations. These can be used to help orient yourself and to confirm your location.
5. Follow the right signs: Many Arctic trails are marked with signs such as ribbons, markers, and paint. Follow these signs to stay on track, and avoid getting lost in the Arctic.
6. Be prepared for emergency: The Arctic environment can be harsh and unforgiving, so it is important to be prepared for an emergency. Make sure to bring a first-aid kit, a signal whistle, a flashlight, and other essentials. Also, let someone know your plan and when to expect you back.
7. Be respectful of the environment: Remember that the Arctic is a fragile ecosystem, and it's essential to minimize your impact on the environment. Stick to established trails and campsites, and don't leave any trash behind.
8. Be aware of the effects of cold on your body: The cold weather can cause hypothermia and frostbite, make sure to be aware of the signs and take precautions to keep your body warm.

- Navigation and orienteering in urban environments

Navigation and orienteering in urban environments can be a bit more challenging than in rural or wilderness areas, but it is still possible to find your way around with the right knowledge and tools. Here are a few tips on how to navigate and orient yourself in an urban environment:

- Learn the layout of the area: Before you set out, try to familiarize yourself with the layout of the area you'll be in. This might include looking at maps, studying street plans, and noting landmarks such as buildings, parks, and bodies of water.
- Use a compass: A compass is a valuable tool for orienteering. It can help you determine your cardinal direction and stay on course.
- Look for landmarks: Landmarks can be used as reference points when navigating. This can be as simple as noting the direction of a tall building, or a large statue.
- Use your phone: Most smartphones come with built-in GPS, which can be very useful for navigation in urban environments. You can use apps such as Google Maps or Apple Maps to get directions and find your way around.
- Follow the crowd: If you're unsure of the way, you can often find your way by following the crowd. People are generally heading in the same direction and it can give you a clue as to where you are headed.
- Pay attention to street signs: Street signs can also be a useful tool for navigation. They can give you information about the name of the street, one-way traffic, and other important information.

III. Crafting for Survival

- **Making tools and weapons**

Making tools and weapons is a crucial survival skill that can help you to acquire food, build shelter, and defend yourself in survival situations. In this chapter, we will cover various techniques for making tools and weapons in different environments and situations.

Section 1: Basic Materials for Tool and Weapon Making

- Identifying and collecting materials for making tools and weapons

To make tools and weapons, you will need to gather and identify materials that are suitable for the task. Some common materials used for making tools and weapons include:

- Stone: Flint, chert, obsidian, and other types of rock can be chipped or flaked to make knives, spears, and other sharp tools.
- Wood: Wood can be used to make spears, arrows, clubs, and other types of weapons. It can also be used to make handles for tools such as axes and hammers.
- Metal: Metals such as copper, bronze, iron, and steel can be used to make a wide variety of tools and weapons, including knives, swords, axes, and more.
- Bone: Bones from animals can be used to make knives, awls, and other tools.
- Fiber: Plant fibers such as flax, hemp, or bark can be used to make cordage, which can be used to make bows, traps, and other tools.

When identifying and collecting materials, it is important to consider the properties of the materials, such as strength, durability, and ease of shaping. It is also important to gather materials in a sustainable and ethical manner.

- Understanding the properties of different materials and how to work with them
-

- Understanding the properties of different materials and how to work with them is an important aspect of making tools and weapons. Each material has its own unique properties that make it suitable for certain tasks and not others. Here are some examples of common materials and their properties:
- Stone: Different types of stone have varying degrees of hardness, which determines how easily they can be shaped. Flint, for example, is relatively hard and brittle, making it good for flaking into sharp edges. Obsidian, on the other hand, is extremely sharp and brittle and is often used to make knives and other cutting tools.
- Wood: Wood is a strong and durable material that can be easily shaped when wet. It is also relatively light, making it a good choice for weapons such as spears and arrows. However, wood can be damaged by rot and insects, so it is important to use wood from a dry and healthy tree.
- Metal: Metals are strong and durable, making them good choices for weapons such as swords and axes. They can also be shaped and hardened through a process called heat treatment. However, metals can rust or corrode if not properly cared for.
- Bone: Bone is a strong and durable material that is relatively easy to shape. It is also lightweight, making it a good choice for tools such as knives and awls. However, bone can be brittle and may break if not handled carefully.
- Fiber: Plant fibers are strong and durable when twisted together, making them a good choice for cordage. Different fibers have different properties and may be more suitable for different tasks. For example, hemp is stronger than flax but less flexible, making it a good choice for bow strings, while flax is more flexible making it better for fishing lines.
- When working with materials, it is important to understand their properties and how to shape them. This may involve using different tools and techniques such as flaking, knapping, carving, grinding, and polishing.
-
- Using natural materials, found materials, and improvised materials

Using natural materials, found materials, and improvised materials can be a great way to make tools and weapons without the need for modern technology or resources. Here are a few examples of how you might use these materials:

- Natural materials: Many natural materials can be used to make tools and weapons. For example, you can use a piece of flint to make a knife, or a straight stick to make a spear. You can also use plants such as nettles or thistles to make cordage, or animal hides to make clothing or shelter.
- Found materials: You can also use found materials to make tools and weapons. For example, you could use a discarded piece of metal pipe to make a spear, or a broken bottle to make a knife. You can also use everyday items such as nails, screws, and wire to make tools and weapons.
- Improvised materials: You can also improvise tools and weapons using materials that are not typically used for that purpose. For example, you could use a rock tied to a stick to make a hammer, or a piece of metal or plastic to make a saw.

When using natural, found, or improvised materials, it is important to consider the properties of the materials and how to work with them. It is also important to use the materials in a sustainable and ethical manner.

It is also important to note that you should be familiar with the laws, regulations and safety measures in your area, some materials may not be legal to possess or use as weapons.

Making tools and weapons from natural, found, or improvised materials can be a challenging but rewarding task. Here are a few tips on how to make different types of tools and weapons:

- Knives: To make a knife, you'll need a piece of sharp-edged material such as flint, obsidian, or steel. You can shape the edge by flaking, knapping, or grinding. A handle can be made from wood, bone, or antler.
- Spears: To make a spear, you'll need a long, straight shaft such as a wooden pole or metal pipe. The spearhead can be made from a

sharpened stone, metal, or glass. To attach the spearhead to the shaft, you can use cordage, sinew, or wire.
- Bows and arrows: To make a bow, you'll need a flexible piece of wood such as yew or osage orange. The bowstring can be made from plant fibers such as hemp or flax. To make arrows, you'll need straight wooden shafts and arrowheads made from stone, metal, or glass. Feathers can be used for fletching to improve the arrow's flight.
- Hammers: To make a hammer, you can use a large rock or piece of metal as the head and attach it to a wooden handle using cordage, sinew, or wire.
- Fishing gear: To make a fishing line, you can use plant fibers such as flax or hemp. To make a fishing hook, you can use a bent wire or a bone. A fishing weight can be made from a small rock or a piece of metal.

- Making knives

Making a knife from natural, found, or improvised materials can be a challenging but rewarding task. Here are a few tips on how to make a knife:

- Choose the right material: The most important part of making a knife is choosing the right material for the blade. Good options include flint, obsidian, or high carbon steel.
- Shape the blade: Once you have the material for the blade, you'll need to shape it. This can be done by flaking, knapping, or grinding. The edge should be as sharp as possible.
- Handle: The handle can be made from a variety of materials such as wood, bone, or antler. It should be comfortable to hold and provide a secure grip.
- Attach the blade to the handle: The blade needs to be securely attached to the handle. This can be done using cordage, sinew, or wire.
- Sharpen and maintain: The knife will require sharpening and maintenance to keep it in good condition. A honing stone can be used to sharpen the edge, and oil can be used to protect the blade

from rust.

It's also important to note that knives can be dangerous, and you should be familiar with knife safety and the laws, regulations and safety measures in your area, some knives may not be legal to possess or use.

Additionally, it's important to note that making a knife with natural, found, or improvised materials may not be as effective or durable as those made with modern tools and materials. It's also important to consider the laws, regulations and safety measures in your area, some materials or tools may not be legal to possess or use.

ction 2: Tool-making TechniquesMaking knives and spears

- Making axes and hatchets

Making an axe or hatchet from natural, found, or improvised materials can be a challenging but rewarding task. Here are a few tips on how to make an axe or hatchet:

- Choose the right material: The most important part of making an axe or hatchet is choosing the right material for the blade. Good options include flint, obsidian, or high carbon steel.
- Shape the blade: Once you have the material for the blade, you'll need to shape it. This can be done by flaking, knapping, or grinding. The edge should be as sharp as possible and the shape of the blade should match the desired use of the axe or hatchet
- Handle: The handle can be made from a variety of materials such as wood, bone, or antler. It should be strong enough to withstand the force of chopping and provide a secure grip.
- Attach the blade to the handle: The blade needs to be securely attached to the handle. This can be done using cordage, sinew, or wire. A wooden handle can be carved to fit the shape of the blade, and then glued and pinned or wedged in place.
- Sharpen and maintain: The axe or hatchet will require sharpening and maintenance to keep it in good condition. A honing stone can be used to sharpen the edge, and oil can be used to protect the blade

from rust.

Additionally, it's important to note that making an axe or hatchet with natural, found, or improvised materials may not be as effective or durable as those made with modern tools and materials. It's also important to consider the laws, regulations and safety measures in your area, some materials or tools may not be legal to possess or use.

- Making hammers and saws

Making a hammer or saw from natural, found, or improvised materials can be a challenging but rewarding task. Here are a few tips on how to make a hammer or saw:

- Choose the right material: The most important part of making a hammer or saw is choosing the right material for the head or blade. Good options for the hammer head include flint, rock, or high carbon steel, and for saws, you can use a hardwood, or a piece of metal.
- Shape the head or blade: Once you have the material for the head or blade, you'll need to shape it. This can be done by flaking, knapping, or grinding. The edge should be as sharp as possible and the shape of the head or blade should match the desired use of the hammer or saw.
- Handle: The handle can be made from a variety of materials such as wood, bone, or antler. It should be strong enough to withstand the force of striking or cutting and provide a secure grip.
- Attach the head or blade to the handle: The head or blade needs to be securely attached to the handle. This can be done using cordage, sinew, or wire. A wooden handle can be carved to fit the shape of the head or blade, and then glued and pinned or wedged in place.
- Sharpen and maintain: The hammer or saw will require sharpening and maintenance to keep it in good condition. A honing stone can be used to sharpen the edge, and oil can be used to protect the blade from rust.

It's also important to note that hammers and saws can be dangerous, and you should be familiar with their safety and the laws, regulations and safety measures in your area, some hammers and saws may not be legal to possess or use.

Additionally, it's important to note that making a hammer or saw with natural, found, or improvised materials may not be as effective or durable as those made with modern tools and materials. It's also important to consider the laws, regulations and safety measures in your area, some materials or tools may not be legal to possess or use.

- Making traps and snares

Making traps and snares from natural, found, or improvised materials can be a useful survival skill. Here are a few tips on how to make traps and snares:

- Choose the right location: The first step in making a trap or snare is to choose the right location. Look for areas where animals are known to travel or forage, such as near a water source or along game trails.
- Understand the behavior of the animal: It's important to understand the behavior of the animal you're trying to trap or snare. This will help you choose the right type of trap or snare and set it in the right location.
- Use the right materials: The materials you use to make a trap or snare will depend on the type of animal you're trying to catch and the environment you're in. Common materials include cordage, wire, or fishing line for the noose, and branches, sticks, or rocks for the structure of the trap.
- Set the trap or snare: Once you have the materials, you'll need to set the trap or snare. This can involve digging a hole, building a trigger mechanism, or attaching the noose to a tree or other anchor point.
- Check and maintain the traps regularly: It's important to check your traps and snares regularly to ensure they are functioning properly, to remove any caught animal, and to ensure that the trap is not causing harm to any non-targeted animals.

Note that traps and snares can be dangerous, and you should be familiar with the laws, regulations and safety measures in your area, some traps and snares may not be legal to possess or use. Additionally, it's important to consider the ethical implications of trapping and snaring, as it can cause harm to animals and the ecosystem. If you're not sure about the laws, regulations and safety measures in your area, it's best to consult with the relevant authorities.

- Making fishing gear

Making fishing gear from natural, found, or improvised materials can be a challenging but rewarding task. Here are a few tips on how to make fishing gear:

- Choose the right location: The first step in making fishing gear is to choose the right location. Look for areas where fish are known to swim, such as near a river, lake, or ocean.
- Understand the behavior of the fish: It's important to understand the behavior of the fish you're trying to catch. This will help you choose the right type of fishing gear and set it in the right location.
- Use the right materials: The materials you use to make fishing gear will depend on the type of fish you're trying to catch and the environment you're in. Common materials include cordage, wire, or fishing line for the line, and branches, sticks, or rocks for the structure of the fishing gear.
- Make the fishing gear: Once you have the materials, you'll need to make the fishing gear. This can involve making a fishing rod or spear, a fishing net, or a fishing trap.
- Check and maintain the fishing gear regularly: It's important to check your fishing gear regularly to ensure they are functioning properly and to ensure that the fishing gear is not causing harm to any non-targeted fish or marine life.

It's also important to note that making fishing gear with natural, found, or improvised materials may not be as effective or durable as those made with modern tools and materials. It's also important to consider the laws, regulations and safety measures in your area, some materials or tools may not be legal to possess or use. Additionally, it's important to consider the ethical implications of fishing and the regulations regarding the size and number of fish that can be caught, and the seasons of fishing. If you're not sure about the laws, regulations and safety measures in your area, it's best to consult with the relevant authorities.

- Making containers and baskets

Making containers and baskets from natural, found, or improvised materials can be a useful skill for storing and transporting items. Here are a few tips on how to make containers and baskets:

- Choose the right materials: The materials you use to make a container or basket will depend on the environment you're in. Common materials include willow, birch, reed, or other types of flexible, pliable branches or grasses.
- Prepare the materials: Before you begin making your container or basket, you'll need to prepare the materials by stripping off any leaves or bark and soaking them in water to make them more pliable.
- Learn basic techniques: There are several basic techniques for making a container or basket, including coiling, plaiting, and twining. These techniques involve wrapping or twisting the materials around each other to create a sturdy structure. It's important to learn and practice these techniques before trying to make a container or basket.
- Assemble the container or basket: Once you have the materials and techniques ready, you can begin assembling the container or basket. This can involve creating a base, then building up the sides, and securing the materials with stitches or knots.
- Add a handle or strap: If you want to be able to carry your container or basket, you'll need to add a handle or strap. This can be done by attaching a piece of cordage or a strip of leather to the top of the container or basket.

Making containers and baskets with natural, found, or improvised materials may not be as effective or durable as those made with modern tools and materials. Additionally, it's important to consider the laws, regulations and safety measures in your area, and the ethical implications of using certain natural materials, like protected species of plants or animals. If you're not sure about the laws, regulations and safety measures in your area, it's best to consult with the relevant authorities.

Section 3: Weapon-making Techniques

- Making bows and arrows

Making bows and arrows from natural, found, or improvised materials can be a challenging but rewarding task. Here are a few tips on how to make bows and arrows:

- Choose the right materials: The materials you use to make a bow and arrows will depend on the environment you're in. Common materials for bows include wood, such as yew, ash, or maple, and for arrows, wood or reed.
- Understand the mechanics of a bow: It's important to understand the mechanics of a bow in order to make one that is functional and efficient. A bow is a spring that stores energy and releases it to propel the arrow forward. The energy stored in the bow is determined by the strength and elasticity of the materials used, and the shape and length of the bow.
- Make the bow: Once you have the materials, you'll need to make the bow. The process of making a bow typically involves shaping the wood into a curved shape, attaching a bowstring, and tuning the bow to achieve the desired draw weight and arrow velocity.
- Make the arrow: Once the bow is ready, you can start making the arrows. The process of making an arrow typically involves selecting the right kind of wood or reed for the shaft, attaching fletching(feathers) for stabilization and adding a point or tip to the arrowhead.
- Check and maintain the bow and arrows regularly: It's important to

check your bow and arrows regularly to ensure they are functioning properly and to ensure that they are not causing harm to any non-targeted creatures or property.

Making bows and arrows with natural, found, or improvised materials may not be as effective or durable as those made with modern tools and materials. Additionally, it's important to consider the laws, regulations and safety measures in your area, and the ethical implications of using a bow and arrow for hunting or other purposes. If you're not sure about the laws, regulations and safety measures in your area, it's best to consult with the relevant authorities.

- Making slingshots and blowguns

Making slingshots and blowguns from natural, found, or improvised materials can be a fun and useful skill. Here are a few tips on how to make slingshots and blowguns:

- Choose the right materials: The materials you use to make a slingshot or blowgun will depend on the environment you're in. Common materials for slingshots include wood, rubber bands, and metal or plastic forks. Common materials for blowguns include bamboo, PVC pipe, or metal tubing.
- Make the slingshot: Once you have the materials, you can start making the slingshot. The process typically involves shaping the wood into a Y-shape, attaching rubber bands to the arms of the Y, and securing a pocket or pouch to hold the ammunition (such as marbles or steel balls).
- Make the blowgun: To make a blowgun, you will need to select the right size and type of tubing and make sure it is smooth and straight. Then, you will need to make a mouthpiece or dart holder at the end of the tube, where you can insert and blow the dart.
- Make darts: To make darts, you can use materials such as bamboo skewers, wooden dowels, or metal wire. You will need to sharpen one end and make a fletching(feathers) at the other end to stabilize the dart while in flight.

- Check and maintain the slingshot and blowgun regularly: It's important to check your slingshot and blowgun regularly to ensure they are functioning properly and to ensure that they are not causing harm to any non-targeted creatures or property.

Making slingshots and blowguns with natural, found, or improvised materials may not be as effective or durable as those made with modern tools and materials. Additionally, it's important to consider the laws, regulations and safety measures in your area, and the ethical implications of using a slingshot or blowgun for hunting or other purposes. If you're not sure about the laws, regulations and safety measures in your area, it's best to consult with the relevant authorities.

- Making traps and snares for hunting

Making traps and snares for hunting from natural, found, or improvised materials can be a useful survival skill. Here are a few tips on how to make traps and snares:

- Choose the right materials: The materials you use to make a trap or snare will depend on the environment you're in and the type of animal you're trying to catch. Common materials include wood, cordage (such as paracord or natural fibers), and metal or plastic wire.
- Understand the mechanics of the trap or snare: It's important to understand the mechanics of the trap or snare in order to make one that is functional and efficient. Traps and snares are designed to capture an animal by either holding it in place or restraining it.
- Make the trap or snare: Once you have the materials, you can start making the trap or snare. The process typically involves creating a trigger mechanism, such as a bent sapling, or a simple loop or noose that will hold the animal.
- Place the trap or snare: It's important to place the trap or snare in an area where the targeted animal is known to travel or forage.
- Check and maintain the trap or snare regularly: It's important to check your trap or snare regularly to ensure they are functioning

properly and to ensure that they are not causing harm to any non-targeted creatures or property.

It's also important to note that making traps and snares with natural, found, or improvised materials may not be as effective or durable as those made with modern tools and materials. Additionally, it's important to consider the laws, regulations and safety measures in your area, and the ethical implications of using traps and snares for hunting or other purposes. If you're not sure about the laws, regulations and safety measures in your area, it's best to consult with the relevant authorities.

- Making spears and other thrusting weapons

Making spears and other thrusting weapons from natural, found, or improvised materials can be a useful survival skill. Here are a few tips on how to make a spear:

- Choose the right materials: The materials you use to make a spear will depend on the environment you're in. Common materials include wood, metal or plastic pipe, or bamboo. You will also need a sharp point, which can be made from stone, metal, or bone.
- Make the spear: Once you have the materials, you can start making the spear. The process typically involves shaping the shaft of the spear, attaching the point to the shaft, and adding a handle or grip to the shaft.
- Add a fire-hardening technique for wooden spears: This process involves heating the spear tip and allowing it to cool quickly, making the wood harder and more durable.
- Make other thrusting weapons: other thrusting weapons can be made with similar materials and methods, such as the lance, the pike and the spear-dagger.
- Check and maintain the spear: It's important to check your spear regularly to ensure it is in good condition and to sharpen the point if necessary.

It's also important to note that making spears and other thrusting weapons with natural, found, or improvised materials may not be as effective or durable as those made with modern tools and materials. Additionally, it's important to consider the laws, regulations and safety measures in your area, and the ethical implications of using a spear for hunting or other purposes. If you're not sure about the laws, regulations and safety measures in your area, it's best to consult with the relevant authorities.

- Making clubs and other striking weapons

Making clubs and other striking weapons from natural, found, or improvised materials can be a useful survival skill. Here are a few tips on how to make a club:

- Choose the right materials: The materials you use to make a club will depend on the environment you're in. Common materials include wood, metal pipes, or heavy branches.
- Make the club: Once you have the materials, you can start making the club. The process typically involves shaping the club to the desired size and shape, adding a handle or grip to the shaft, and possibly adding a weight or a knob to one end of the club to increase its impact.
- Add a fire-hardening technique for wooden clubs: This process involves heating the club and allowing it to cool quickly, making the wood harder and more durable.
- Make other striking weapons: Other striking weapons can be made with similar materials and methods, such as the mace, the flail, and the warhammer.
- Check and maintain the club: It's important to check your club regularly to ensure it is in good condition, and to make sure the handle or grip is securely attached to the shaft.

Making clubs and other striking weapons with natural, found, or improvised materials may not be as effective or durable as those made with modern tools and materials. Additionally, it's important to consider the laws, regulations and safety measures in your area, and the ethical implications of using a club for hunting or other purposes. If you're not sure about the laws, regulations and safety measures in your area, it's best to consult with the relevant authorities.

Section 4: Tool and Weapon Making in Different Environments

- Making tools and weapons in the desert

Making tools and weapons in a desert environment can be a challenging task, as the materials available may be limited and the harsh conditions can make it difficult to work with them. Here are a few tips on how to make tools and weapons in the desert:

- Look for natural materials: In a desert environment, natural materials such as cactus, palm fronds, and desert willows can be used to make tools and weapons. You can also look for materials such as stones, bones, and metal debris that may have been left behind by previous inhabitants or travelers.
- Use the sun to harden materials: In the absence of fire, you can use the sun to harden materials such as wood or resin. Leave the material in the sun during the hottest part of the day and it will dry out and become harder.
- Use sand and rocks to sharpen edges: You can use sand and rocks to sharpen edges of tools and weapons. Place the edge of the tool against a rock or a piece of sandstone, and rub it back and forth to sharpen it.
- Make traps and snares: Desert animals are often adapted to the harsh conditions, so making traps and snares can be a good way to catch food. Look for natural materials such as cactus, palm fronds, or branches to make traps, and use the desert's natural features such as rocks or dunes to conceal them.
- Make a water container: A water container can be made using materials such as cactus, hides, or even plastic bags.

- Making tools and weapons in the jungle

Making tools and weapons in a jungle environment can be a challenging task, as the materials available may be limited and the humid conditions can make it difficult to work with them. Here are a few tips on how to make tools and weapons in the jungle:

- Look for natural materials: In a jungle environment, natural materials such as bamboo, hardwoods, and vines can be used to make tools and weapons. You can also look for materials such as stones, bones, and metal debris that may have been left behind by previous inhabitants or travelers.
- Use hardwoods: Hardwoods such as teak, rosewood, and hickory are strong and durable, and can be used to make tools and weapons that can withstand the humidity and heavy use.
- Use the jungle's natural features: The jungle environment offers many natural features that can be used to make tools and weapons, such as large leaves, thorns, and shells.
- Make traps and snares: Jungle animals are often adapted to the dense forest, so making traps and snares can be a good way to catch food. Look for natural materials such as vines, branches, or leaves to make traps, and use the jungle's natural features such as trees or rocks to conceal them.
- Make a water container: A water container can be made using materials such as bamboo, coconut shells, or even plastic bags.

- Making tools and weapons in the arctic

Making tools and weapons in an arctic environment can be challenging, as the materials available may be limited and the cold conditions can make it difficult to work with them. Here are a few tips on how to make tools and weapons in the arctic:

- Look for natural materials: In an arctic environment, natural materials such as bone, antler, and ivory can be used to make tools and weapons. You can also look for materials such as stones and metal debris that may have been left behind by previous inhabitants or travelers.

- Use animal hides: Animal hides from arctic animals such as caribou, muskox, and seal can be used to make clothing, footwear, and other items that can help keep you warm.
- Use the snow and ice: Snow and ice can be used to make tools and weapons, such as ice picks and ice axes. You can also use snow to insulate shelter and to make blocks for building igloos.
- Make traps and snares: Arctic animals are often adapted to the cold conditions, so making traps and snares can be a good way to catch food. Look for natural materials such as branches, willow, or grass to make traps, and use the arctic's natural features such as rocks or snowdrifts to conceal them.
- Make a fire: Fire is essential for survival in the arctic, and it can be used to melt snow and ice for drinking water, as well as to cook food and dry clothing.

- Making tools and weapons in urban environments

Making tools and weapons in an urban environment can be challenging, as the materials available may be limited and the legal and safety considerations may be stricter than in other environments. Here are a few tips on how to make tools and weapons in an urban environment:

- Look for found materials: In an urban environment, found materials such as metal pipes, screws, nails, and other debris can be used to make tools and weapons.
- Use common household items: Common household items such as scissors, kitchen knives, and hammers can be used as tools and weapons in an emergency situation.
- Make improvised weapons: In an urban environment, it may be necessary to make improvised weapons such as pepper spray, tasers, or even a slingshot using found materials.
- Be aware of laws and regulations: It's important to be aware of the laws and regulations regarding weapons and tools in your area, as they may vary depending on your location. It may be illegal to carry

certain items or to make certain types of weapons.
- Safety considerations: Always consider the safety implications of any tools or weapons you make, both for yourself and for others. Improvised weapons can be dangerous if not handled properly and can lead to serious injury or even death.

- **Building traps and snares**

Traps and snares are an essential part of survival in many environments, as they can provide a reliable source of food and help protect you from dangerous animals. In this chapter, we will cover the basics of building traps and snares, including:

- Understanding the different types of traps and snares and their suitability for different environments and animals

Traps and snares are devices used to capture or immobilize animals for hunting, pest control, or wildlife management purposes. The type of trap or snare used will depend on the target animal, the environment, and the purpose of the trapping.

Some common types of traps and snares include:

- Conibear traps: These are body-gripping traps that are designed to quickly and humanely kill the target animal. They are commonly used for trapping small to medium-sized mammals such as raccoons, muskrats, and beavers.
- Leghold traps: These are traps that hold the animal by the leg, they are not legal in some countries and states, they are banned in Europe since the 80's. These are used to capture larger mammals such as foxes, coyotes, and bobcats.
- Live traps: These are traps that are designed to capture the animal without killing it, they are used for wildlife management and research, to relocate or study the animal. These can be used for a variety of animals, from small mammals like squirrels and raccoons to larger animals like bears and deer.

- Snares: These are loops of wire or cable that are designed to tighten around the animal's neck or body when triggered. They are commonly used for trapping small mammals, birds, and reptiles.
- Pitfall traps: These are traps that are dug into the ground and covered with a removable lid. When an animal falls into the pit, it is unable to escape. They are often used for catching small mammals, reptiles, and amphibians.

- Identifying and collecting materials for building traps and snares

Building traps and snares typically requires a variety of materials, depending on the type of trap or snare you are constructing. Some common materials that may be used include:

- Wire: This can be used to construct snares and to reinforce other trap components. It can be made from various materials such as steel, copper or stainless steel, and it can come in different gauges depending on the animal you are trapping.
- Rope or cordage: This is used to construct triggers, tie down stakes, and construct snares. It can be made from natural fibers such as hemp or manila, or synthetic fibers such as nylon or paracord.
- Wood: This is used to construct the frame of many types of traps, such as live traps and some snares. It should be strong enough to hold the animal and must be able to resist rot and decay.
- Metal: This is used to construct some of the mechanical parts of traps, such as springs and triggers. It should be rust-resistant and strong enough to hold the animal.
- Natural materials: This can include leaves, grass, and branches, which are used to camouflage the trap and make it less visible to the target animal.
- Lures and baits: These are used to attract the target animal to the trap or snare. Lures can be used to lure the animal to a specific location, while baits can be used to entice the animal to enter the trap or snare.

- Understanding the principles of trap and snare design

The principles of trap and snare design involve understanding the behavior of the target animal and using that knowledge to create a trap or snare that will effectively capture or immobilize the animal. Some key principles to consider when designing a trap or snare include:

- Trigger: The trigger is the mechanism that sets off the trap or snare. It should be sensitive enough to detect the target animal, but not so sensitive that it is triggered by non-target animals or the environment.
- Holding power: The trap or snare should be strong enough to hold the animal once it is triggered. This is particularly important for live traps, which must be able to contain the animal without injuring it.
- Camouflage: The trap or snare should be concealed from the target animal as much as possible. This can be done by using natural materials to camouflage the trap or by placing it in a location where the animal is unlikely to notice it.
- Placement: The trap or snare should be placed in a location where the target animal is known to travel or where it is likely to find food or shelter.
- Lures and baits: Lures and baits can be used to attract the target animal to the trap or snare. These should be chosen based on the animal's natural diet or preferences.
- Safety: The trap or snare should be designed to be safe for the target animal, non-target animals, and people. It should be easy to check and maintain without risking injury.
- Legal requirements: It's important to research and comply with all laws and regulations regarding trapping in your area, as certain types of traps and snares may be restricted or prohibited.

- Understanding the importance of location and placement when building traps and snares

Location and placement are critical factors in the success of a trap or snare. The trap or snare should be placed in a location where the target animal is known to travel or where it is likely to find food or shelter. This will increase the chances of the animal encountering the trap or snare and being captured.

When choosing a location for a trap or snare, it's important to consider the following factors:

- Animal activity: The trap or snare should be placed in an area where the target animal is known to be active. This can include areas where the animal is known to forage for food or travel through.
- Natural features: The trap or snare should be placed near natural features that the animal is likely to use, such as water sources, shelter, or food sources.
- Accessibility: The trap or snare should be placed in an area that is easy to access, so that it can be checked and maintained regularly.
- Safety: The trap or snare should be placed in a location that is safe for the target animal, non-target animals, and people.
- Legal requirements: Some areas may have specific laws and regulations regarding trapping, it's important to research and comply with all laws and regulations regarding trapping in your area.

In addition to location, the placement of the trap or snare is also important. The trap or snare should be placed in a position that will maximize the chances of the animal encountering it and being captured. This can include placing the trap or snare in a natural pathway that the animal is likely to use, or in an area where the animal is likely to forage for food.

Section 1: Basic Traps and Snares

- Building deadfall traps

A deadfall trap is a type of trap that uses a heavy object, known as a deadfall, to kill or immobilize the target animal. These traps are typically used to catch small mammals and birds, and can be constructed using a variety of materials.

Here are the basic steps for building a deadfall trap:

1. Gather materials: You will need a heavy object for the deadfall, such as a large rock or log, as well as sticks or poles for the frame of the trap. You may also want to use cord or wire to secure the trap.

2. Build the frame: Use the sticks or poles to construct a triangular frame for the trap. The frame should be sturdy and able to support the weight of the deadfall.
3. Add the trigger: The trigger is the mechanism that releases the deadfall when the animal takes the bait. A simple trigger can be made by using a stick or pole that rests on the frame and supports the deadfall. The stick or pole should be placed in such a way that the slightest movement of the bait will cause it to release the deadfall.
4. Add the deadfall: Place the heavy object (deadfall) on top of the frame and secure it in place using cord or wire.
5. Add bait: Place the bait on top of the frame, near the trigger, to attract the target animal to the trap.
6. Conceal and camouflage the trap: Cover the trap with leaves or other natural materials to conceal it from the target animal and its surroundings.
7. Check the trap regularly and dispose of any animals caught humanely.

- Building figure-four triggers

A figure-four trigger, also known as a figure-four deadfall, is a type of trigger used in deadfall traps. It is a more advanced trigger mechanism that allows for a smaller deadfall to be used, and it also increases the chances of a successful capture.

Here are the basic steps for building a figure-four trigger for a deadfall trap:

1. Gather materials: You will need two sticks or poles, one for the upright and one for the crosspiece, as well as cord or wire to secure the trigger.
2. Build the upright: Take one of the sticks or poles and make a "V" shape by cutting a small notch at the top of the stick, this will be the upright.
3. Build the crosspiece: Take the second stick or pole and make a small notch at one end, this will be the crosspiece.
4. Assemble the trigger: Place the crosspiece on top of the upright, so

that the notch in the crosspiece sits in the "V" of the upright. The crosspiece should be able to rotate freely on top of the upright.
5. Add the trigger stick: Take a third stick and place it underneath the crosspiece, so that one end of the stick is resting on the ground and the other end is resting against the crosspiece. This stick will be used to release the deadfall when the animal takes the bait.
6. Secure the trigger: Use cord or wire to secure the trigger in place, making sure that the crosspiece can rotate freely on top of the upright.
7. Set the trap: Place the deadfall on top of the trigger and bait the trap.
8. Conceal and camouflage the trap: Cover the trap with leaves or other natural materials to conceal it from the target animal and its surroundings.
9. Check the trap regularly and dispose of any animals caught humanely.

- Building spring snares

A spring snare is a type of trap that uses a spring-loaded mechanism to quickly close around an animal's neck or body when triggered. These snares are typically used to catch small mammals and birds, and can be constructed using a variety of materials.

Here are the basic steps for building a spring snare:

1. Gather materials: You will need a spring-loaded mechanism, such as a bent sapling or a spring-loaded trap, as well as cord or wire to create the noose and secure the trap.
2. Set the spring-loaded mechanism: Place the spring-loaded mechanism in the location where you want to set the snare. The mechanism should be anchored securely to the ground or a nearby tree or stake.
3. Create the noose: Use cord or wire to create a noose that will be placed around the animal's neck or body. The noose should be large enough to allow the animal to move freely, but small enough to close quickly when the animal is caught.

4. Attach the noose to the spring-loaded mechanism: Use cord or wire to attach the noose to the spring-loaded mechanism. Make sure the noose is positioned correctly and that the spring-loaded mechanism is in the locked position.
5. Add bait: Place bait near the snare to attract the target animal to the trap.
6. Conceal and camouflage the trap: Cover the trap with leaves or other natural materials to conceal it from the target animal and its surroundings.
7. Check the trap regularly and dispose of any animals caught humanely.

- Building bow traps

A bow trap, also known as a bow trigger or bow-catch trap, is a type of trap that uses a bent sapling or a piece of flexible wood as the trigger mechanism. The trap is triggered when an animal pulls on the bait, causing the bent sapling to straighten out and release the catch.

Here are the basic steps for building a bow trap:

1. Gather materials: You will need a flexible sapling or a piece of wood, cord or wire to secure the trap, and bait to attract the animal.
2. Bend the sapling: Take the flexible sapling or piece of wood and bend it into a "U" shape. The sapling should be bent to a point where it is under tension and will straighten out when triggered.
3. Secure the sapling: Use cord or wire to secure the sapling in place, making sure that it is under tension and will straighten out when triggered.
4. Set the catch: Place the catch, such as a stick or rock, on top of the sapling. The catch should be positioned so that it will be released when the sapling straightens out.
5. Add the bait: Place bait near the trap to attract the target animal to the trap.
6. Conceal and camouflage the trap: Cover the trap with leaves or other natural materials to conceal it from the target animal and its

surroundings.
7. Check the trap regularly and dispose of any animals caught humanely.

- Building fish traps

Fish traps are devices used to catch fish in a variety of aquatic environments. There are many different types of fish traps, but they all work by using bait to attract fish into an enclosed area where they can be easily caught.

Here are the basic steps for building a simple fish trap:

1. Gather materials: You will need materials such as bamboo, mesh or wire, and bait to attract the fish.
2. Construct the frame: Using the materials you have gathered, construct a frame for the trap. The frame should be large enough to hold several fish and should be able to be securely sealed.
3. Add the mesh or wire: Securely attach the mesh or wire to the frame. The mesh or wire should be small enough to prevent the fish from escaping but large enough to allow water to flow through.
4. Add the bait: Place the bait inside the trap where it can be easily reached by the fish.
5. Place the trap in the water: Place the trap in the desired location, making sure it is anchored securely.
6. Check the trap regularly: Fish trapped inside the trap should be removed and properly dispatched as soon as possible.

- Building bird snares

Building a bird snare is illegal in most places, it's also considered inhumane and it's not recommended. Birds are protected by laws and regulations, and it's important to respect and follow them. Hunting or trapping birds without a permit can result in fines and other penalties.

I recommend to not build bird snares and instead, consider alternative methods such as bird feeders, bird houses and bird baths to attract birds to your property. This can provide a safe and enjoyable way to observe birds in their natural habitat.

Section 2: Advanced Traps and Snares

- Building pitfall traps

A pitfall trap is a type of trap that uses a deep hole to capture small animals such as insects, amphibians, and reptiles. The trap is triggered when an animal falls into the hole and is unable to escape.

Here are the basic steps for building a pitfall trap:

1. Gather materials: You will need a digging tool, a container or bucket, a cover (such as a piece of plywood), and bait or a lure to attract the target animals.
2. Dig the hole: Using your digging tool, dig a hole that is deep enough to capture the target animals, but not so deep that they cannot be removed. The hole should be at least 6 inches deep and wide enough to accommodate the container or bucket.
3. Place the container: Place the container or bucket inside the hole. Make sure the rim of the container is level with the ground.
4. Add the bait or lure: Place bait or a lure inside the container to attract the target animals.
5. Cover the trap: Place the cover over the hole and container, making sure it is secure and stable.
6. Check the trap regularly: Check the trap every few hours, and remove any animals that have been captured. Be sure to handle the animals carefully and release them in a safe and appropriate location.
7. Conceal the trap: Cover the trap with leaves or other natural materials to conceal it from the target animal and its surroundings.

- Building snare traps for large animals

Building a snare trap for large animals is not recommended as it is illegal in most places and considered inhumane. Large animals such as deer, elk, and big game animals are protected by laws and regulations, and it's important to respect and follow them. Hunting or trapping large animals without a permit can result in fines and other penalties.

Additionally, snares are not considered a safe or humane way to trap large animals. These animals are strong and can easily break free from a snare, or worse, get injured in the process. Additionally, snares can also capture non-target animals and cause harm to them.

If you need to control the population of large animals on your property, it's best to consult with a professional wildlife biologist or a local wildlife agency for safe and humane methods. They will be able to provide you with the appropriate guidelines and tools to control the population of large animals in a humane way.

- Building camouflage and concealment techniques

Camouflage and concealment are important techniques used to hide traps and snares from both the target animals and potential human observers. These techniques can help to increase the effectiveness of the trap or snare and reduce the chances of detection.

Here are a few basic techniques for building camouflage and concealment for traps and snares:

1. Use natural materials: Gather natural materials such as leaves, branches, and grass to cover and conceal the trap or snare. This will help it blend in with the surrounding environment.
2. Use camouflage netting: Camouflage netting can be used to cover the trap or snare, helping it blend in with the surrounding environment.
3. Use paint or dye: Paint or dye can be used to match the trap or snare to the surrounding environment.
4. Use a blind: A blind is a structure that can be used to conceal the trap or snare. This can be made from natural materials or camouflage netting.
5. Use the topography: Take advantage of natural features such as rocks, trees, and bushes to conceal the trap or snare.
6. Conceal the trap with plants: Use plants to cover the trap, but be careful not to use poisonous plants.

7. Position the trap or snare in a natural way: Position the trap or snare in a way that looks natural, such as a deer trail or a beaver dam.

- Building traps and snares in water

Building traps and snares in water can be an effective way to catch fish and other aquatic animals, but it is important to understand the unique challenges and considerations that come with trapping in this environment.

Here are a few tips for building traps and snares in water:

1. Use appropriate materials: Use materials that are resistant to rust and corrosion, such as stainless steel or aluminum, as they will last longer in the water.
2. Consider water flow: Be aware of the flow and currents in the water and position the trap or snare accordingly. Fish and other aquatic animals tend to move with the flow of the water, so the trap or snare should be placed in an area where the flow will bring them towards it.
3. Use natural bait: Fish and other aquatic animals are attracted to natural bait, such as worms, insects, or small fish.
4. Use a funnel: A funnel-shaped trap or snare can help to guide the fish or other aquatic animals into the trap.
5. Use fish traps: Fish traps are a common method for catching fish. They can be made from various materials such as bamboo, wood or metal. These traps can be baited with a variety of baits and are placed in the water.
6. Use a gill net: A gill net is a type of fishing net that is set in the water to catch fish by the gills. It can be set in a variety of ways, such as anchored to the bottom or suspended in the water.
7. Be aware of regulations: Be sure to check local regulations regarding trapping in water and obtain any necessary permits.

Section 3: Traps and Snares in Different Environments

- Building traps and snares in the desert

Building traps and snares in the desert can be challenging due to the harsh conditions and limited resources, but it is possible with the right knowledge and materials.

Here are a few tips for building traps and snares in the desert:

1. Use natural materials: Gather natural materials such as cacti, rocks, and sand to conceal the trap or snare. This will help it blend in with the surrounding environment.
2. Use the topography: Take advantage of natural features such as rocks, dunes, and cliffs to conceal the trap or snare.
3. Use the animals tracks: Position the trap or snare in an area where animals are known to travel, such as near a watering hole or along a game trail.
4. Use the sun's position: Position the trap or snare so that it is in the shade during the hottest part of the day. This will help to keep the trap or snare cool and reduce the chance of animals detecting it by smell.
5. Use natural bait: Use natural baits that are known to attract the animals you are trying to trap, such as seeds, fruits, or insects.
6. Use deadfall traps: Deadfall traps are effective in the desert. They are easy to build and can be used to catch small mammals and reptiles.
7. Be aware of regulations: Be sure to check local regulations regarding trapping in the desert and obtain any necessary permits.

- Building traps and snares in the jungle

Building traps and snares in the jungle can be challenging due to the dense vegetation, high humidity, and diverse wildlife, but it is possible with the right knowledge and materials.

Here are a few tips for building traps and snares in the jungle:

1. Use natural materials: Gather natural materials such as vines, branches, and leaves to conceal the trap or snare. This will help it blend in with the surrounding environment.
2. Use the topography: Take advantage of natural features such as rivers,

creeks, and cliffs to conceal the trap or snare.
3. Use the animals tracks: Position the trap or snare in an area where animals are known to travel, such as near a watering hole or along a game trail.
4. Use the natural bait: Use natural baits that are known to attract the animals you are trying to trap, such as fruits, insects, or small animals.
5. Use deadfall traps: Deadfall traps are effective in the jungle. They are easy to build and can be used to catch small mammals and reptiles.
6. Use spring snares: Spring snares can be used to catch a variety of animals, such as small mammals, birds, and reptiles.
7. Be aware of regulations: Be sure to check local regulations regarding trapping in the jungle and obtain any necessary permits.

It's important to note that these techniques should be used in conjunction with legal and ethical trapping practices. It's important to check all traps and snares regularly and release any non-target animals unharmed. It is also important to be aware of the risks of injury or disease while working in the jungle, like snakes, leeches, and tropical diseases. It is always recommended to have a professional guide or get the appropriate training before trying to trap in the jungle.

- Building traps and snares in the arctic

Building traps and snares in the Arctic can be challenging due to the harsh weather conditions, limited resources, and the migratory nature of many Arctic animals. However, it is possible with the right knowledge and materials.

Here are a few tips for building traps and snares in the Arctic:

1. Use natural materials: Gather natural materials such as ice, snow, and branches to conceal the trap or snare. This will help it blend in with the surrounding environment.
2. Use the topography: Take advantage of natural features such as rivers, creeks, and cliffs to conceal the trap or snare.
3. Use the animals tracks: Position the trap or snare in an area where animals are known to travel, such as near a watering hole or along a

game trail.
4. Use the natural bait: Use natural baits that are known to attract the animals you are trying to trap, such as fish, berries or small animals.
5. Use deadfall traps: Deadfall traps are effective in the Arctic. They are easy to build and can be used to catch small mammals and reptiles.
6. Use spring snares: Spring snares can be used to catch a variety of animals, such as small mammals, birds, and reptiles.
7. Be aware of regulations: Be sure to check local regulations regarding trapping in the Arctic and obtain any necessary permits.

- Building traps and snares in urban environments

Building traps and snares in urban environments is generally not recommended, as it is illegal in most cases and can be dangerous to both animals and people. Additionally, many urban animals, such as pigeons, rats, and raccoons, have become accustomed to human presence and may not be caught by traditional traps and snares.

Instead, if you need to address a problem with urban wildlife, it is best to contact a professional wildlife control service. They will be able to identify the specific animal and determine the most appropriate and humane solution. If you are looking to trap animals on your property, it is important to check your local regulations and obtain the necessary permits before doing so.

Furthermore, it is important to use humane methods of control and avoid killing or injuring animals, as well as, avoiding to create more problems than the ones you are trying to solve.

- **Creating clothing and footwear**

Creating clothing and footwear is an essential survival skill that can help you to stay warm, dry, and protected in harsh environments. In this chapter, we will cover the basics of creating clothing and footwear, including:

- Understanding the importance of layering and insulation in clothing

Layering and insulation are important factors to consider when dressing for cold weather, as they help to trap heat close to the body and protect against the elements. Layering involves wearing multiple layers of clothing, each with a specific function, to create a system that can be adjusted as needed.

The three main layers of clothing are:

1. Base layer: This layer is worn closest to the skin and is designed to wick moisture away from the body. It is typically made of synthetic materials such as polyester or merino wool.
2. Insulating layer: This layer is worn over the base layer and is designed to trap heat and keep the body warm. It is typically made of materials such as down, synthetic fibers, or fleece.
3. Outer layer: This layer is worn over the insulating layer and is designed to protect against wind and precipitation. It is typically made of materials such as Gore-Tex, or other breathable and waterproof fabrics.

By layering, you can adjust your clothing to suit the temperature and activity level. For example, if you're engaging in a high-intensity activity, such as skiing, you'll likely need to wear less insulation to prevent overheating. However, if you're sitting still, you'll need more insulation to keep warm.

- Identifying and collecting materials for creating clothing and footwear

When creating clothing and footwear, there are many different materials that can be used depending on the desired function and style. Some common materials used for clothing and footwear include:

1. Cotton: a natural fiber that is breathable, soft, and easy to dye. It is often used for t-shirts, pants, and other casual clothing.
2. Wool: a natural fiber that is warm, insulating, and moisture-wicking. It is often used for sweaters, socks, and other cold-weather clothing.
3. Synthetic fibers: such as polyester, nylon, and spandex. These fibers are lightweight, quick-drying, and often used in activewear, outdoor gear, and technical clothing.

4. Leather: a durable and water-resistant material that is often used for footwear and outdoor gear.
5. Canvas: a durable and heavy-duty material that is often used for outdoor gear, bags, and footwear.
6. Rubber: a waterproof and durable material that is often used for boots and other outdoor footwear.
7. Down: a natural insulation made from the plumage of geese and ducks. It's used in jackets and sleeping bags

When collecting materials for creating clothing and footwear, it is important to consider the intended use and desired properties of the final product. Some materials may be more suitable for certain types of clothing or footwear, and it is important to choose materials that will work well together. Additionally, you should consider the availability and cost of the materials, and the skill level required to work with them.

- Understanding the principles of clothing and footwear design

The principles of clothing and footwear design involve understanding the human body, the function and performance of different materials, and the aesthetics and trends of fashion.

1. Human anatomy and ergonomics: Clothing and footwear designers must have a good understanding of the human body and how it moves in order to create garments that fit well and are comfortable to wear. This includes understanding body proportions, measurements, and how different fabrics and construction techniques can affect fit and comfort.
2. Materials and fabrication: Choosing the right materials and fabrication techniques is crucial for creating clothing and footwear that will perform well and meet the intended function. Designers must understand the properties of different fabrics and materials and how they can be manipulated to create different styles and effects. They must also understand the different types of construction techniques and how they can be used to create different types of

garments and footwear.
3. Aesthetics and trends: Clothing and footwear design is also about creating visually appealing and fashionable items. Designers must stay current with the latest fashion trends and be able to create garments that are visually appealing, while also meeting the performance and function requirements.
4. Branding and Marketing: Designers must be aware of the market and target audience they are designing for, and design garments and footwear that will appeal to those groups. They should also be aware of the branding and marketing strategies of the company they are working for and design garments that align with those strategies
5. Sustainability: Clothing and footwear designers must consider the environmental and social impact of their designs and materials choices. This may include using sustainable or organic materials, reducing waste and energy consumption in production, and designing garments that are made to last.

- Understanding the importance of fit, comfort, and functionality when creating clothing and footwear

Fit, comfort, and functionality are crucial aspects of clothing and footwear design.

1. Fit: A well-fitting garment or footwear item is one that is proportionate to the body and allows for ease of movement. This means that the garment should be cut to the correct size and shape, and should not be too tight or too loose. A good fit can also enhance the appearance of the wearer and make them feel more confident.
2. Comfort: Comfort is an essential aspect of clothing and footwear design. Garments and footwear that are uncomfortable to wear will not be worn for long. Designers must consider the materials and construction techniques used in their designs to ensure that the final product is comfortable to wear. This includes considering factors such as fabric weight, breathability, and stretch.
3. Functionality: Clothing and footwear must also be functional and

meet the needs of the intended use. For example, outdoor clothing and footwear must be designed to protect the wearer from the elements, while athletic clothing and footwear must be designed to support and enhance performance. Designers must also consider factors such as durability, ease of movement, and protection when designing clothing and footwear for specific activities or environments.
4. Layering: Layering is an important aspect of clothing and footwear design, particularly for outdoor and cold weather clothing. Layering allows the wearer to adjust their clothing to suit different temperatures and weather conditions. Designers must consider how different layers will interact and how they can be used to create a system that will keep the wearer warm and dry.

In summary, clothing and footwear design must take into account the fit, comfort and functionality of the garments and footwear. This includes understanding the human anatomy and ergonomics, the materials and fabrication techniques, the aesthetics and trends, and the layering and insulation principles.

Section 1: Basic Clothing and Footwear

- Making shirts, pants, and other garments from natural fibers

To make shirts, pants, and other garments from natural fibers, you will need natural fabric such as cotton, linen, or wool, a sewing machine or needle and thread, and a pattern or design for the garment.

First, cut the fabric to the desired size and shape using the pattern or design as a guide. Then, sew the edges of the fabric together to create the basic shape of the garment.

Next, add any additional features such as pockets, buttons, or zippers. You may also want to add a lining for added warmth or comfort.

Finally, make sure that all seams are secure and that the garment has a finished look by hemming the edges, adding a collar or cuffs, etc.

Keep in mind that natural fibers need special care, like hand-washing or dry cleaning. Also, natural fibers like cotton and linen need to be pre-shrunk before cutting and sewing.

- Making ponchos and other waterproof garments

To make a poncho or other waterproof garment, you will need a waterproof fabric such as Gore-Tex or nylon, a sewing machine or needle and thread, and a pattern or design for the garment.

First, cut the fabric to the desired size and shape using the pattern or design as a guide. Then, sew the edges of the fabric together to create the basic shape of the garment.

Next, add any additional features such as a hood or a zipper. If the garment will be worn in cold weather, you may also want to add a lining for warmth.

Finally, make sure that all seams are sealed to prevent water from seeping through. You can seal the seams by using a seam sealer or by applying a thin layer of waterproofing agent to the inside of the garment.

Note: Some fabrics are already waterproof and breathable, so you don't need to add any additional sealer.

- Making mittens, gloves, and other hand coverings

To make mittens, gloves, and other hand coverings, you will need a fabric such as wool, fleece, or a waterproof-breathable fabric, a sewing machine or needle and thread, and a pattern or design for the hand covering.

First, cut the fabric to the desired size and shape using the pattern or design as a guide. Then, sew the edges of the fabric together to create the basic shape of the hand covering.

Next, add any additional features such as a thumb hole, a closure (such as a button or a velcro), or a lining for added warmth.

Make sure that all seams are secure and that the hand covering has a finished look by hemming the edges, adding a cuff or trim.

If you're using a waterproof-breathable fabric, you should also seal the seams to prevent water from seeping through.

Note that if you're making mittens, you'll need to make two separate pieces for each mitten and then sew them together leaving an opening for the thumb.

- Making hats, hoods, and other head coverings

To make hats, hoods, and other head coverings, you will need a fabric such as wool, fleece, or a waterproof-breathable fabric, a sewing machine or needle and thread, and a pattern or design for the head covering.

First, cut the fabric to the desired size and shape using the pattern or design as a guide. Then, sew the edges of the fabric together to create the basic shape of the head covering.

Next, add any additional features such as a brim, a visor, or a drawstring closure. If the head covering will be worn in cold weather, you may also want to add a lining for added warmth.

Make sure that all seams are secure and that the head covering has a finished look by hemming the edges, adding a binding or trim.

If you're using a waterproof-breathable fabric, you should also seal the seams to prevent water from seeping through.

Also, you may want to consider adding a chin strap or elastic band to keep the hat in place, especially for windy conditions.

Note that if you're making hoods, you'll need to attach it to a jacket or a coat.

- Making shoes, sandals, and other footwear from natural materials

Making shoes, sandals, and other footwear from natural materials can be a challenging task as it requires a combination of skills such as sewing, leatherworking, and possibly even cobbling. Here's a general outline of the process:

1. First, gather the necessary materials such as leather, canvas, rubber, or other natural materials.
2. Next, create a pattern for the shoe or sandal, taking into account the desired fit and style.
3. Cut the leather or other materials to the pattern.

4. Assemble the shoe or sandal by sewing or gluing the pieces together.
5. Apply any additional features such as laces, buckles, or straps.
6. Finish the shoe or sandal by attaching a sole, made of rubber, leather or other materials.
7. Treat the leather with an appropriate conditioner to protect it from water and other elements.

Keep in mind that making footwear from natural materials requires a significant amount of time and skill, and it may be difficult for a beginner. It's a good idea to start with simple designs and work your way up to more complex ones.

Section 2: Advanced Clothing and Footwear

- Making clothing and footwear from animal hides

Making clothing and footwear from animal hides is a traditional technique that requires specific skills, tools, and materials. Here's a general outline of the process:

1. First, obtain the hides from a reputable source. The hides should be properly tanned and treated to make them suitable for use in clothing and footwear.
2. Next, create a pattern for the clothing or footwear, taking into account the desired fit and style.
3. Cut the hide to the pattern.
4. Assemble the clothing or footwear by sewing or lacing the pieces together.
5. Apply any additional features such as buttons, zippers, or buckles.
6. Finish the clothing or footwear by attaching a sole, if it's footwear.
7. Treat the hide with an appropriate conditioner to protect it from water and other elements.

Keep in mind that working with animal hides requires a significant amount of skill and experience, and it may be difficult for a beginner. It's a good idea to start with simple designs and work your way up to more complex ones.

- Making clothing and footwear from synthetic materials

Making clothing and footwear from synthetic materials is a common practice in modern fashion and can be done using a sewing machine or a needle and thread. Here's a general outline of the process:

1. First, gather the necessary materials such as synthetic fabrics, thread, and any other embellishments.
2. Next, create a pattern for the clothing or footwear, taking into account the desired fit and style.
3. Cut the fabric to the pattern.
4. Assemble the clothing or footwear by sewing the pieces together, using a sewing machine or a needle and thread.
5. Apply any additional features such as zippers, buttons, or Velcro closures.
6. Finish the clothing or footwear by adding any final touches, such as hems or cuffs.
7. It's not necessary to treat synthetic materials as they are generally resistant to water and other elements.

Keep in mind that the type of synthetic fabric you use will determine the properties of the final product. Some synthetic fabrics are good for making waterproof and breathable clothing, others for moisture-wicking and quick-drying properties, others for stretch and durability.

- Making clothing and footwear from plant fibers

Making clothing and footwear from plant fibers is a traditional technique that has been used for thousands of years. Plant fibers can be used to make a wide variety of clothing and footwear such as linen, cotton, hemp, jute, etc. Here's a general outline of the process:

1. First, gather the necessary materials such as plant fibers, thread, and any other embellishments.
2. Next, create a pattern for the clothing or footwear, taking into account the desired fit and style.

3. Prepare the plant fibers by cleaning, carding, spinning and weaving them.
4. Cut the fabric to the pattern.
5. Assemble the clothing or footwear by sewing the pieces together, using a sewing machine or a needle and thread.
6. Apply any additional features such as zippers, buttons, or Velcro closures.
7. Finish the clothing or footwear by adding any final touches, such as hems or cuffs.

Keep in mind that the type of plant fibers you use will determine the properties of the final product. Some plant fibers like linen and hemp are strong and durable, others like cotton are soft and breathable.

- Making clothing and footwear from recycled materials

Making clothing and footwear from recycled materials is a way to reduce waste and promote sustainability in the fashion industry. The process of making clothing and footwear from recycled materials generally involves collecting and repurposing old textiles, such as clothes and other fabrics. Here's a general outline of the process:

1. First, gather the necessary materials such as old clothes, fabrics, thread, and any other embellishments.
2. Next, create a pattern for the clothing or footwear, taking into account the desired fit and style.
3. Sort and clean the old clothes and fabrics, removing any stains or damage.
4. Cut the fabric to the pattern.
5. Assemble the clothing or footwear by sewing the pieces together, using a sewing machine or a needle and thread.
6. Apply any additional features such as zippers, buttons, or Velcro closures.
7. Finish the clothing or footwear by adding any final touches, such as hems or cuffs.

Keep in mind that when working with recycled materials, it's important to consider the quality and condition of the materials, as well as the original colors and patterns. This can limit the design options, but it also allows you to be creative with repurposing and upcycling.

Section 3: Clothing and Footwear in Different Environments

- Making clothing and footwear for cold weather

Making clothing and footwear for cold weather requires using materials that can provide insulation and protection from the elements such as wind and snow. Here's a general outline of the process:

1. First, gather the necessary materials such as insulated fabrics, waterproof and breathable membranes, zippers, snaps, Velcro, thread, and any other embellishments.
2. Next, create a pattern for the clothing or footwear, taking into account the desired fit and style.
3. Cut the fabric to the pattern.
4. Assemble the clothing or footwear by sewing the pieces together, using a sewing machine or a needle and thread.
5. Apply any additional features such as zippers, snaps, or Velcro closures.
6. Insulate the clothing or footwear by adding a layer of insulation such as down or synthetic fibers
7. Apply any waterproof and breathable membranes to the clothing or footwear.
8. Finish the clothing or footwear by adding any final touches, such as hems or cuffs.

Keep in mind that the type of materials you use will determine the properties of the final product. Insulated fabrics are good for keeping you warm, but some can be heavy and bulky. Waterproof and breathable membranes will keep you dry, but they can make the clothing or footwear less breathable.

- Making clothing and footwear for wet weather

Making clothing and footwear for wet weather requires using materials that can provide protection from the elements such as rain and water. Here's a general outline of the process:

1. First, gather the necessary materials such as waterproof and breathable fabrics, zippers, snaps, Velcro, thread, and any other embellishments.
2. Next, create a pattern for the clothing or footwear, taking into account the desired fit and style.
3. Cut the fabric to the pattern.
4. Assemble the clothing or footwear by sewing the pieces together, using a sewing machine or a needle and thread.
5. Apply any additional features such as zippers, snaps, or Velcro closures.
6. Apply any waterproof and breathable membranes to the clothing or footwear.
7. Finish the clothing or footwear by adding any final touches, such as hems or cuffs.

Keep in mind that the type of materials you use will determine the properties of the final product. Waterproof and breathable fabrics will keep you dry, but they can make the clothing or footwear less breathable.

It's also important to consider the design and construction of the clothing or footwear, as well as the intended use and activity level. For example, if you're making clothing or footwear for heavy rain, you'll want to use materials that are highly waterproof, and have a design that allows for a full range of motion, and drainage of the water.

- Making clothing and footwear for hot weather

Making clothing and footwear for hot weather requires using materials that can provide breathability and ventilation to keep the wearer cool and comfortable. Here's a general outline of the process:

1. First, gather the necessary materials such as lightweight, breathable fabrics, thread, and any other embellishments.

2. Next, create a pattern for the clothing or footwear, taking into account the desired fit and style.
3. Cut the fabric to the pattern.
4. Assemble the clothing or footwear by sewing the pieces together, using a sewing machine or a needle and thread.
5. Apply any additional features such as zippers, snaps, or Velcro closures.
6. Finish the clothing or footwear by adding any final touches, such as hems or cuffs.

- Making clothing and footwear for urban environments

- **Building and maintaining equipment**

Building and maintaining equipment is an essential survival skill that can help you to stay organized, efficient, and effective in any situation. In this chapter, we will cover the basics of building and maintaining equipment, including:

- Understanding the importance of equipment in survival

Equipment is an essential aspect of survival because it can provide the means for shelter, warmth, communication, navigation, and protection. Without the proper equipment, survival in a wilderness or other hostile environment can be extremely difficult, if not impossible.

1. Shelter: Equipment such as tents, tarps, and sleeping bags can provide protection from the elements, including rain, wind, and extreme temperatures. A shelter is necessary for survival as it can keep you dry and warm, which can prevent hypothermia and exposure-related illnesses.
2. Warmth: Equipment such as warm clothing, blankets, and fire-starting tools can help keep the body warm in cold environments. Without warmth, hypothermia can set in and can lead to serious injury or death.
3. Communication: Equipment such as radios, satellite phones, or

signaling devices can help connect you to the outside world and allow you to call for help in an emergency.
4. Navigation: Equipment such as maps, compasses, and GPS devices can help you navigate and find your way in unfamiliar territory. Knowing how to navigate and find your way can be essential to survival.
5. Protection: Equipment such as knives, axes, and firearms can be used for self-defense and protection from wild animals.
6. Food and water: Equipment such as water filters, purifiers, and containers can help provide clean water, while equipment such as fishing and hunting gear, traps, and cooking equipment can help provide food.

It's important to note that having the equipment is not enough, you must also know how to properly use and maintain it. In addition, having a good knowledge of survival skills such as shelter building, fire-starting, navigation, and first aid is also crucial in case of emergency.

In summary, Equipment is an essential aspect of survival. It can provide the means for shelter, warmth, communication, navigation, and protection, and knowing how to properly use and maintain it can mean the difference between life and death in a wilderness or other hostile environment.

- Identifying and collecting materials for building and maintaining equipment

Identifying and collecting materials for building and maintaining equipment is a crucial step in the process of survival. The materials you gather will depend on the specific equipment you need to build or maintain, as well as the environment in which you find yourself. Here are some general steps and tips to help you with identifying and collecting materials:

1. Assess your needs: Before you begin collecting materials, it's important to have a clear idea of what you need. This will help you focus your efforts and ensure that you gather the materials you need to build and maintain your equipment.

2. Study your environment: Observe the environment around you and take note of the natural materials that are available. Look for trees, rocks, plants, and other materials that can be used to build and maintain equipment.
3. Identify useful materials: Once you've studied your environment, you can start identifying useful materials. For example, you may find that certain trees have strong and durable wood that can be used for building shelter, or that certain plants have fibers that can be used for making rope.
4. Gather materials: Once you've identified useful materials, it's time to gather them. Use tools such as a saw, axe, or knife to collect wood, and use your hands to gather smaller materials such as plants and rocks.
5. Store and transport materials: Once you've gathered your materials, it's important to store and transport them in a way that will ensure they stay in good condition. For example, you may need to dry wet wood before using it, or protect your materials from the elements.
6. Keep an inventory of materials: Keeping track of what materials you have and how much of each is important. This will help you plan for future projects and make sure you have enough materials when you need them.
7. Recycle or repurpose equipment: Before discarding broken or worn out equipment, consider if it can be repurposed or recycled. Many items can be fixed with a few modifications or repairs, thus avoiding the need to look for new materials.
8. Learn to improvise: Finally, it's important to learn how to improvise. Sometimes, you may not be able to find the exact materials you need, so it's important to be able to adapt and make do with what you have available.

- Understanding the principles of equipment design

Understanding the principles of equipment design is important in order to create functional and efficient equipment. Here are some key principles to consider when designing equipment:

1. Functionality: The equipment should be designed to perform the specific task or function for which it is intended. It should be easy to use, maintain and repair.
2. Safety: The equipment should be designed with safety in mind. It should not pose a risk of injury to the user or others, and should be designed to meet relevant safety standards.
3. Durability: The equipment should be designed to withstand the conditions in which it will be used. It should be able to withstand wear and tear, as well as exposure to the elements.
4. Ergonomics: The equipment should be designed to be comfortable and easy to use for the user. It should be easy to grip, hold, and operate, and should not cause strain or fatigue.
5. Efficiency: The equipment should be designed to be as efficient as possible. It should use minimal energy or resources to perform its function, and should not waste materials or energy.
6. Maintainability: The equipment should be designed in a way that makes it easy to maintain and repair. It should be easy to access and replace parts, and should not require specialized tools or skills to maintain.
7. Scalability: The equipment should be designed in a way that allows it to be easily scaled up or down depending on the needs of the user.
8. Cost-effectiveness: The equipment should be designed in a way that makes it cost-effective to produce and use. It should not be overly complex or require expensive materials or production methods.
9. Adaptability: The equipment should be designed in a way that allows it to adapt to different environments and situations.
10. Sustainability: The equipment should be designed with sustainability in mind. It should be made of durable, long-lasting materials and should not have a negative impact on the environment.

By keeping these principles in mind, you will be able to design equipment that is functional, safe, durable, efficient, and easy to maintain, adapt and not harmful to the environment.

- Understanding the importance of maintenance and repair when it comes to equipment

Understanding the importance of maintenance and repair when it comes to equipment is crucial for ensuring that the equipment remains in good working condition and continues to perform its intended function. There are several key reasons why maintenance and repair are important:

1. Safety: Regular maintenance and repair can help to ensure that the equipment is safe to use. This includes checking for and addressing any potential safety hazards, such as worn or damaged parts.
2. Longevity: Proper maintenance and repair can help to extend the lifespan of the equipment. This can include regular cleaning and lubrication, as well as addressing any issues that may arise, such as wear and tear.
3. Performance: Regular maintenance and repair can help to ensure that the equipment continues to perform its intended function effectively. This includes checking for and addressing any issues that may affect the equipment's performance, such as worn or damaged parts.
4. Cost-effectiveness: Regular maintenance and repair can help to reduce the overall cost of ownership for the equipment. This includes reducing the need for costly repairs, as well as preventing the need to replace the equipment prematurely.
5. Compliance: Regular maintenance and repair can help to ensure that the equipment meets relevant safety and regulatory standards. This can include ensuring that the equipment is in compliance with relevant occupational health and safety regulations.
6. Sustainability: Regular maintenance and repair can help to ensure that the equipment is environmentally friendly, by reducing the need for frequent replacements and disposals of the equipment.
7. Reliability: Proper maintenance and repair can help to ensure that the equipment is reliable, by keeping the equipment in good working order and reducing the likelihood of breakdowns.

By keeping these factors in mind, you can ensure that your equipment remains in good working condition and continues to perform its intended function effectively, safely, environmentally friendly, reliable and in compliance with regulations.

Section 1: Basic Equipment

- Building backpacks and other carrying equipment

Building backpacks and other carrying equipment can be a challenging task, as it requires a good understanding of the materials, tools, and techniques involved, as well as an understanding of the principles of equipment design.

1. Materials: When building a backpack or other carrying equipment, the first step is to select the right materials. Common materials used include nylon, canvas, leather, and other durable fabrics. It's important to choose materials that are suitable for the intended use of the backpack and that can withstand the elements and wear and tear.
2. Tools: The next step is to gather the necessary tools. This may include a sewing machine, scissors, needles, thread, and other tools and supplies.
3. Design: The design of the backpack is an important factor to consider. This includes factors such as the size and shape of the backpack, the number and location of pockets and compartments, and the placement of straps and other carrying features.
4. Pattern: After the design of the backpack is complete, the next step is to create a pattern. This can be done by cutting and measuring the materials and then creating a template for the backpack.
5. Sewing: Once the pattern is complete, the next step is to sew the backpack together. This will typically involve attaching the straps, pockets, and other features to the main body of the backpack.
6. Finishing: The last step is to finish the backpack. This includes adding any final touches, such as adding zippers, buckles, or other hardware.
7. Inspection: After the backpack is complete, it's important to inspect the backpack to ensure that it is safe and functional, and that it meets the design specifications.

8. Maintenance: After the backpack is in use, regular maintenance and repair will be necessary to ensure the backpack remains in good working condition and continues to perform its intended function effectively, safely and in compliance with regulations.

Building backpacks and other carrying equipment requires a certain level of skill and experience, and it's essential to understand the materials, tools, and techniques involved, as well as the principles of equipment design. With the right knowledge and experience, it's possible to create a high-quality backpack or other carrying equipment that is both functional and durable.

- Building shelters and other structures

Building shelters and other structures is an important part of survival, as it provides protection from the elements and other environmental hazards. There are several factors to consider when building a shelter or other structure, including materials, design, and location.

1. Materials: The materials used to build a shelter will depend on the environment and the intended use of the shelter. Common materials include wood, stone, mud, and other natural materials that can be found in the local area.
2. Design: The design of the shelter is also an important factor to consider. This includes factors such as the shape and size of the shelter, the number and location of openings, and the placement of structural elements such as supports and beams.
3. Location: The location of the shelter is also an important consideration. Factors to consider include the availability of materials, the proximity to water and other resources, and the exposure to sun, wind, and other environmental hazards.
4. Planning: Before beginning to build the shelter, it's important to plan and prepare. This might involve gathering materials, creating a design, and marking out the location of the shelter.
5. Building: Once the planning and preparation is complete, the next step is to begin building the shelter. This will typically involve

clearing the site, laying a foundation, and building the walls and roof.
6. Finishing: After the shelter is built, the next step is to finish the shelter. This might involve adding a door, windows, or other features to make the shelter more comfortable and functional.
7. Inspection: After the shelter is complete, it's important to inspect the shelter to ensure that it is safe and functional, and that it meets the design specifications.
8. Maintenance: After the shelter is in use, regular maintenance and repair will be necessary to ensure the shelter remains in good working condition and continues to perform its intended function effectively, safely and in compliance with regulations.

- Building tools and weapons

Building tools and weapons is an important aspect of survival, as it allows you to gather resources, defend yourself, and perform a variety of tasks. There are several factors to consider when building tools and weapons, including materials, design, and functionality.

1. Materials: The materials used to build tools and weapons will depend on the environment and the intended use of the tool or weapon. Common materials include wood, stone, metal, and other natural materials that can be found in the local area.
2. Design: The design of the tool or weapon is also an important factor to consider. This includes factors such as the shape, size, and weight of the tool or weapon, as well as the placement and type of any sharp edges or points.
3. Functionality: The intended use of the tool or weapon is also an important consideration. For example, a knife will have a different design and materials than a spear or bow.
4. Planning: Before beginning to build the tool or weapon, it's important to plan and prepare. This might involve gathering materials, creating a design, and practicing the skills needed to create the tool or weapon.
5. Building: Once the planning and preparation is complete, the next

step is to begin building the tool or weapon. This will typically involve shaping and sharpening the materials, attaching any handles or other components, and testing the tool or weapon to ensure it is functional and safe.
6. Finishing: After the tool or weapon is built, the next step is to finish the tool or weapon. This might involve adding a handle, sheath, or other features to make the tool or weapon more comfortable and functional.
7. Inspection: After the tool or weapon is complete, it's important to inspect the tool or weapon to ensure that it is safe and functional, and that it meets the design specifications.
8. Maintenance: After the tool or weapon is in use, regular maintenance and repair will be necessary to ensure the tool or weapon remains in good working condition and continues to perform its intended function effectively, safely and in compliance with regulations.

- Building lighting equipment

Building lighting equipment is an important aspect of survival, as it allows you to see in low-light conditions and navigate in the dark. There are several factors to consider when building lighting equipment, including materials, design, and functionality.

1. Materials: The materials used to build lighting equipment will depend on the environment and the intended use of the light. Common materials include wood, metal, glass, and other natural materials that can be found in the local area.
2. Design: The design of the lighting equipment is also an important factor to consider. This includes factors such as the shape, size, and weight of the light, as well as the placement and type of any lenses or reflectors.
3. Functionality: The intended use of the lighting equipment is also an important consideration. For example, a flashlight will have a different design and materials than a lantern or campfire.
4. Planning: Before beginning to build the lighting equipment, it's

important to plan and prepare. This might involve gathering materials, creating a design, and practicing the skills needed to create the lighting equipment.
5. Building: Once the planning and preparation is complete, the next step is to begin building the lighting equipment. This will typically involve shaping and attaching the materials, creating lenses or reflectors, and testing the lighting equipment to ensure it is functional and safe.
6. Finishing: After the lighting equipment is built, the next step is to finish the lighting equipment. This might involve adding a handle, switch, or other features to make the lighting equipment more comfortable and functional.
7. Inspection: After the lighting equipment is complete, it's important to inspect the lighting equipment to ensure that it is safe and functional, and that it meets the design specifications.
8. Maintenance: After the lighting equipment is in use, regular maintenance and repair will be necessary to ensure the lighting equipment remains in good working condition and continues to perform its intended function effectively, safely and in compliance with regulations.

Building lighting equipment requires a certain level of skill and experience, and it's essential to understand the materials, tools, and techniques involved, as well as the principles of equipment design. With the right knowledge and experience, it's possible to create high-quality lighting equipment that is both functional and durable.

- Building cooking equipment

Building cooking equipment is an important aspect of survival, as it allows you to prepare food safely and efficiently. There are several factors to consider when building cooking equipment, including materials, design, and functionality.

1. Materials: The materials used to build cooking equipment will

depend on the environment and the intended use of the equipment. Common materials include metal, clay, stone, and other natural materials that can be found in the local area.
2. Design: The design of the cooking equipment is also an important factor to consider. This includes factors such as the shape, size, and weight of the equipment, as well as the placement and type of any flues, vents, or heat sources.
3. Functionality: The intended use of the cooking equipment is also an important consideration. For example, a campfire will have a different design and materials than a stove or oven.
4. Planning: Before beginning to build the cooking equipment, it's important to plan and prepare. This might involve gathering materials, creating a design, and practicing the skills needed to create the cooking equipment.
5. Building: Once the planning and preparation is complete, the next step is to begin building the cooking equipment. This will typically involve shaping and attaching the materials, creating flues or vents, and testing the cooking equipment to ensure it is functional and safe.
6. Finishing: After the cooking equipment is built, the next step is to finish the cooking equipment. This might involve adding a handle, switch, or other features to make the cooking equipment more comfortable and functional.
7. Inspection: After the cooking equipment is complete, it's important to inspect the cooking equipment to ensure that it is safe and functional, and that it meets the design specifications.
8. Maintenance: After the cooking equipment is in use, regular maintenance and repair will be necessary to ensure the cooking equipment remains in good working condition and continues to perform its intended function effectively, safely and in compliance with regulations.

Section 2: Advanced Equipment

- Building communication equipment

Building communication equipment is an important aspect of survival, as it allows you to stay in contact with others and receive information in emergency situations. There are several types of communication equipment that can be built, including radios, signal mirrors, and flares.

1. Radios: Radios can be built using a variety of materials, including metal, plastic, and wood. To build a radio, you will need to have a basic understanding of electrical circuits and be able to work with electronic components such as transistors, capacitors, and resistors.
2. Signal mirrors: Signal mirrors are a simple and effective way to communicate over long distances. They can be made from a variety of materials, including plastic, glass, and metal. To build a signal mirror, you will need to have a basic understanding of optics and be able to shape and polish the mirror surface.
3. Flares: Flares are a powerful signaling tool that can be used to signal for help in emergency situations. They can be made from a variety of materials, including wood, paper, and metal. To build a flare, you will need to have a basic understanding of chemistry and be able to work with materials that burn and produce light.
4. Planning: Before building communication equipment, it's important to plan and prepare. This might involve gathering materials, creating a design, and practicing the skills needed to create the communication equipment.
5. Building: Once the planning and preparation is complete, the next step is to begin building the communication equipment. This will typically involve assembling the parts and testing the equipment to ensure it is functional and safe.
6. Finishing: After the communication equipment is built, the next step is to finish the communication equipment. This might involve adding a handle, switch, or other features to make the communication equipment more comfortable and functional.
7. Inspection: After the communication equipment is complete, it's important to inspect the communication equipment to ensure that it is safe and functional, and that it meets the design specifications.
8. Maintenance: After the communication equipment is in use, regular

maintenance and repair will be necessary to ensure the communication equipment remains in good working condition and continues to perform its intended function effectively, safely and in compliance with regulations.

- Building navigation equipment

Building navigation equipment is an important aspect of survival, as it allows you to determine your location and navigate to safety in emergency situations. There are several types of navigation equipment that can be built, including compasses, sextants, and GPS receivers.

1. Compasses: A compass is a simple and effective navigation tool that can be built using a variety of materials, including metal, plastic, and wood. To build a compass, you will need to have a basic understanding of magnetism and be able to work with materials such as magnets and needles.
2. Sextants: A sextant is a precision navigation tool that can be used to determine your position at sea by measuring the angle between the horizon and a celestial body such as the sun or stars. To build a sextant, you will need to have a basic understanding of optics and be able to work with materials such as mirrors and lenses.
3. GPS receivers: GPS receivers are electronic devices that can be built using a variety of materials, including plastic and metal. To build a GPS receiver, you will need to have a basic understanding of electronics and be able to work with components such as microcontrollers, antennas, and batteries.
4. Planning: Before building navigation equipment, it's important to plan and prepare. This might involve gathering materials, creating a design, and practicing the skills needed to create the navigation equipment.
5. Building: Once the planning and preparation is complete, the next step is to begin building the navigation equipment. This will typically involve assembling the parts and testing the equipment to ensure it is functional and safe.

6. Finishing: After the navigation equipment is built, the next step is to finish the navigation equipment. This might involve adding a handle, switch, or other features to make the navigation equipment more comfortable and functional.
7. Inspection: After the navigation equipment is complete, it's important to inspect the navigation equipment to ensure that it is safe and functional, and that it meets the design specifications.
8. Maintenance: After the navigation equipment is in use, regular maintenance and repair will be necessary to ensure the navigation equipment remains in good working condition and continues to perform its intended function effectively, safely and in compliance with regulations.

- Building water treatment equipment

Building water treatment equipment is a crucial aspect of survival, as it allows you to purify and make safe drinking water in emergency situations. There are several types of water treatment equipment that can be built, including filtration systems, chemical treatment systems, and solar stills.

1. Filtration systems: Filtration systems are designed to remove physical contaminants from water, such as sediment, dirt, and debris. These can be built using a variety of materials, including ceramic, sand, and gravel. To build a filtration system, you will need to have a basic understanding of water flow and be able to work with materials such as PVC pipe and fittings.
2. Chemical treatment systems: Chemical treatment systems use chemicals such as chlorine or iodine to disinfect water and remove harmful pathogens. These can be built using a variety of materials, including plastic bottles and containers, and can be constructed easily.
3. Solar stills: Solar stills use the heat of the sun to distill water and remove impurities. These can be built using materials such as plastic sheeting and tubing, and can be constructed easily.
4. Planning: Before building water treatment equipment, it's important

to plan and prepare. This might involve gathering materials, creating a design, and practicing the skills needed to create the water treatment equipment.
5. Building: Once the planning and preparation is complete, the next step is to begin building the water treatment equipment. This will typically involve assembling the parts and testing the equipment to ensure it is functional and safe.
6. Finishing: After the water treatment equipment is built, the next step is to finish the water treatment equipment. This might involve adding a handle, switch, or other features to make the water treatment equipment more comfortable and functional.
7. Inspection: After the water treatment equipment is complete, it's important to inspect the water treatment equipment to ensure that it is safe and functional, and that it meets the design specifications.
8. Maintenance: After the water treatment equipment is in use, regular maintenance and repair will be necessary to ensure the water treatment equipment remains in good working condition and continues to perform its intended function effectively, safely and in compliance with regulations.

- Building power and energy equipment

Building power and energy equipment is an important aspect of survival, as it allows you to generate electricity and power various devices in emergency situations. There are several types of power and energy equipment that can be built, including solar panels, wind turbines, and hydroelectric generators.

1. Solar panels: Solar panels convert sunlight into electrical energy. These can be built using materials such as silicon, glass, and aluminum, and can be constructed with a moderate level of skill and experience.
2. Wind turbines: Wind turbines harness the power of the wind to generate electricity. These can be built using materials such as steel, aluminum, and plastic, and can be constructed with a moderate level of skill and experience.

3. Hydroelectric generators: Hydroelectric generators harness the power of moving water to generate electricity. These can be built using materials such as steel, aluminum, and plastic, and can be constructed with a moderate level of skill and experience.
4. Planning: Before building power and energy equipment, it's important to plan and prepare. This might involve gathering materials, creating a design, and practicing the skills needed to create the power and energy equipment.
5. Building: Once the planning and preparation is complete, the next step is to begin building the power and energy equipment. This will typically involve assembling the parts and testing the equipment to ensure it is functional and safe.
6. Finishing: After the power and energy equipment is built, the next step is to finish the power and energy equipment. This might involve adding a handle, switch, or other features to make the power and energy equipment more comfortable and functional.
7. Inspection: After the power and energy equipment is complete, it's important to inspect the power and energy equipment to ensure that it is safe and functional, and that it meets the design specifications.
8. Maintenance: After the power and energy equipment is in use, regular maintenance and repair will be necessary to ensure the power and energy equipment remains in good working condition and continues to perform its intended function effectively, safely and in compliance with regulations.

Section 3: Building and maintaining equipment in different environments

- Building and maintaining equipment in the desert

Building and maintaining equipment in the desert can be challenging due to the harsh conditions, including high temperatures, low humidity, and extreme sunlight. Here are a few tips to keep in mind when building and maintaining equipment in the desert:

1. Use materials that can withstand the heat: When building

equipment, use materials that are heat-resistant and can withstand the harsh conditions of the desert. This may include materials such as aluminum, stainless steel, and plastic.
2. Consider the effects of the sun: The sun in the desert can be extremely intense and can cause damage to equipment. When building or maintaining equipment, consider adding shading or reflective materials to help protect it from the sun's rays.
3. Use rust-proof and corrosion-resistant materials: The desert environment can be harsh on equipment due to the dust, sand, and dry air. Use materials that are rust-proof and corrosion-resistant to help protect equipment and prolong its lifespan.
4. Use sealants and lubricants: Sand and dust can easily get into moving parts and cause damage. Use sealants and lubricants to help protect equipment from the desert environment.
5. Regular maintenance: Regular maintenance is crucial to keep equipment in good working condition in the desert. Schedule regular inspections and cleanings to remove dust and sand from equipment and ensure that it is functioning properly.
6. Water: Water is a precious resource in the desert, so it's important to consider how equipment will be used and maintained in relation to water. Some equipment may require water for cooling or other purposes, so it's important to plan for this when building and maintaining equipment.
7. Building shelters: Building shelters in the desert can be challenging due to the heat and lack of materials. Consider using natural materials such as rocks, sand, and vegetation to build a shelter.
8. Avoid building fires: Building fires in the desert can be dangerous and is not recommended, because of the dry and windy conditions. If you need to cook food or generate heat, consider using equipment specifically designed for this purpose, such as a solar cooker or a portable stove.
9. Emergency kits: Always carry an emergency kit with you when traveling in the desert, including a first aid kit, a map, a compass, a flashlight, and a water filter or purification tablets.

- Building and maintaining equipment in the jungle

Building and maintaining equipment in the jungle can be challenging due to the humid and wet conditions, as well as the presence of plants and animals that can damage equipment. Here are a few tips to keep in mind when building and maintaining equipment in the jungle:

1. Use materials that can withstand the humidity: When building equipment, use materials that are resistant to rust and corrosion, such as aluminum, stainless steel, and plastic.
2. Consider the effects of the rain: The jungle is known for its high humidity and frequent rainfalls. Make sure to build equipment that can withstand being wet, use sealants and waterproofing materials when needed.
3. Use rust-proof and corrosion-resistant materials: The jungle environment can be harsh on equipment due to the humidity and wet conditions. Use materials that are rust-proof and corrosion-resistant to help protect equipment and prolong its lifespan.
4. Regular maintenance: Regular maintenance is crucial to keep equipment in good working condition in the jungle. Schedule regular inspections and cleanings to remove dust, mud, and debris from equipment and ensure that it is functioning properly.
5. Building shelters: Building shelters in the jungle can be challenging due to the humidity, rain and lack of materials. Consider using natural materials such as trees, leaves, and vegetation to build a shelter.
6. Avoid building fires: Building fires in the jungle can be dangerous and is not recommended, because of the wet and humid conditions. If you need to cook food or generate heat, consider using equipment specifically designed for this purpose, such as a portable stove.
7. Watch out for pests: The jungle is home to many pests, such as insects and rodents, that can damage equipment. Keep equipment in sealed containers and use pest repellent to keep them away.
8. Watch out for animals: The jungle is home to many animals, such as monkeys and parrots, that can damage equipment. Keep equipment

out of reach and use protective covers when necessary.
9. Emergency kits: Always carry an emergency kit with you when traveling in the jungle, including a first aid kit, a map, a compass, a flashlight, and a water filter or purification tablets.

- Building and maintaining equipment in the arctic

Building and maintaining equipment in the arctic can be challenging due to the extreme cold and harsh conditions. Here are a few tips to keep in mind when building and maintaining equipment in the arctic:

1. Use materials that can withstand the cold: When building equipment, use materials that are resistant to cold and cracking, such as plastic, aluminum, and stainless steel. Avoid materials that are prone to freezing, such as copper and brass.
2. Insulate equipment: Insulation is crucial to keeping equipment from freezing in the arctic. Use insulation materials, such as foam or fiberglass, to protect equipment from the cold.
3. Keep equipment dry: The arctic environment can be harsh on equipment due to the snow, ice, and freezing rain. Make sure to build equipment that can withstand being wet, use sealants and waterproofing materials when needed.
4. Use lubricants that work in the cold: Standard lubricants can freeze in the arctic, which can cause equipment to seize up. Use lubricants that are specifically designed to work in cold temperatures.
5. Regular maintenance: Regular maintenance is crucial to keep equipment in good working condition in the arctic. Schedule regular inspections and cleanings to remove ice and snow from equipment and ensure that it is functioning properly.
6. Building shelters: Building shelters in the arctic can be challenging due to the cold and lack of materials. Consider using natural materials such as snow, ice and vegetation to build a shelter.
7. Watch out for the wind: Wind chill can make the arctic feel much colder than it actually is. Be sure to take wind chill into account when building and maintaining equipment.

8. Build equipment with multiple functions: The arctic environment can be harsh and unforgiving, so building equipment with multiple functions can be a lifesaver in an emergency situation.
9. Emergency kits: Always carry an emergency kit with you when traveling in the arctic, including a first aid kit, a map, a compass, a flashlight, and a water filter or purification tablets.
10. Dress for the weather: Make sure to dress in layers that can be removed or added as needed to stay warm. Wear insulated boots and gloves, a warm hat and a face mask to protect against the wind.

- Building and maintaining equipment in urban environments

Building and maintaining equipment in urban environments can present a different set of challenges than in other environments. Here are a few tips to keep in mind when building and maintaining equipment in an urban environment:

1. Use durable materials: Urban environments can be tough on equipment due to the high level of wear and tear. Use materials that are durable and can withstand heavy use, such as steel, aluminum, and high-density plastics.
2. Use rust inhibitors: Urban environments can be damp and humid which can cause rust to form on equipment. Use rust inhibitors to protect metal parts from rusting.
3. Use vibration dampeners: Urban environments can be noisy and equipment may be exposed to vibration from the traffic and other sources. Use vibration dampeners to reduce the impact of vibration on equipment.
4. Use weather-resistant finishes: Urban environments can be exposed to pollution, dust, and other airborne contaminants. Use weather-resistant finishes to protect equipment from the elements.
5. Use non-marking wheels or casters: Urban environments often have polished or delicate flooring, so use non-marking wheels or casters to prevent damage.
6. Use security features: Urban environments can be prone to theft, so

consider using security features such as locking mechanisms, alarms, or GPS tracking to protect equipment.
7. Regular maintenance: Regular maintenance is crucial to keep equipment in good working condition in urban environments. Schedule regular inspections and cleanings to remove dust, grime, and other contaminants from equipment and ensure that it is functioning properly.
8. Compact design: Urban environments have limited space, so consider building equipment with a compact design to save space.
9. Urban mobility: Urban environments are often crowded and chaotic, so consider building equipment with wheels or casters to make it easy to move around.
10. Power supply: Urban environments often have a limited power supply, so consider building equipment that can operate on batteries or other alternative power sources.

- **Improvised medical treatments**

Advanced survival techniques are designed to help you to stay alive and thrive in extreme environments. In this chapter, we will cover advanced survival techniques that are not covered in previous chapters, including:

- Understanding the importance of advanced survival techniques

Advanced survival techniques are important for individuals who may find themselves in extreme or unexpected survival situations. These techniques can help you to stay alive and healthy in challenging environments and can make the difference between life and death. Some examples of advanced survival techniques include:

1. Navigation: Knowing how to navigate using a map, compass, and other tools can help you to find your way in unfamiliar environments.
2. First aid: Having advanced first aid skills can help you to treat injuries and illnesses that may occur in a survival situation.
3. Water purification: Knowing how to purify water using different

methods can help you to avoid water-borne illnesses and dehydration.
4. Fire-making: Knowing how to make fire using different methods can help you to stay warm, cook food, and signal for help.
5. Shelter-building: Knowing how to build different types of shelters can help you to protect yourself from the elements.
6. Signaling for rescue: Knowing how to signal for rescue using different methods can increase your chances of being found in a survival situation.
7. Foraging and hunting: Knowing how to find and catch food in the wild can help you to stay nourished in a survival situation.
8. Mental and emotional preparation: Knowing how to stay mentally and emotionally strong in a survival situation can help you to stay calm and focused.
9. Knots and rope work: Knowing how to tie different knots and use rope in survival situations can help you to secure your shelter, equipment and make a rescue signal.
10. Survival psychology: Understanding how the human mind and body react in survival situations can help you to prepare for and cope with the physical and emotional challenges of survival.

- Identifying and adapting to different environments

Identifying and adapting to different environments is an important aspect of survival. The environment in which you find yourself will have a significant impact on your ability to survive and thrive. Understanding the specific characteristics of different environments and how they may affect you is key to making good decisions and taking appropriate actions.

Here are some steps to help you identify and adapt to different environments:

1. Observation: Take a close look at the environment around you. Pay attention to the terrain, weather, vegetation, and wildlife. Try to identify any potential hazards and resources.
2. Research: Learn as much as you can about the environment you are in. This can include studying maps, talking to local experts, and

reading books or articles about the area.
3. Planning: Based on the information you have gathered, plan how to best adapt to the environment. This can include choosing the best location for a camp, selecting the appropriate clothing and equipment, and developing a survival strategy.
4. Implementation: Put your plan into action. This can include building a shelter, finding water, and sourcing food.
5. Monitoring: Continuously monitor the environment and your own condition, and make adjustments as necessary.
6. Flexibility: Be ready to adapt to changing conditions, as the environment can change rapidly.

Different environments, such as deserts, jungles, arctic, and urban environments have their own unique challenges, and will require different strategies to survive. It's important to be aware of and prepared for the specific hazards and resources that each environment offers.

Additionally, it's important to be aware of the different cultures and customs of the people living in these environments, as they may have valuable knowledge and skills that can assist you in your survival.

- Understanding the principles of survival medicine

Survival medicine is the knowledge and skills needed to provide medical care in austere and emergency environments where conventional medical resources may not be readily available. Here are some of the key principles of survival medicine:

1. Prioritization: In a survival situation, medical care must be prioritized. Life-threatening conditions such as severe bleeding, broken bones, and airway obstruction should be treated first, while less critical conditions can be treated later.
2. Prevention: The best way to stay healthy in a survival situation is to prevent injuries and illnesses from occurring in the first place. This can include taking preventive measures such as wearing protective gear and avoiding known hazards.

3. Basic Life Support: Knowing how to provide basic life support, such as CPR and first aid, is essential in a survival situation.
4. Hygiene: Maintaining proper hygiene can prevent the spread of infection and illness. This includes cleaning wounds, washing hands and food, and proper sanitation.
5. Wound Management: Properly managing wounds is important to prevent infection and promote healing. This includes cleaning and dressing wounds, and avoiding contamination.
6. Infection Control: preventing and controlling infections is an important part of survival medicine. This includes proper hygiene, sterilization of equipment, and identifying and treating infections early.
7. Pain Management: Pain management is essential to treating injuries and illnesses in a survival situation. This can include using over-the-counter medications, natural remedies, and other techniques to manage pain.
8. Psychological Support: Providing psychological support is an important aspect of survival medicine. This includes providing emotional support, helping to maintain a positive attitude and addressing any mental health concerns.
9. Improvisation: In a survival situation, you may have to improvise with the resources available. This can include using natural materials to make splints or bandages, and using makeshift equipment to treat injuries and illnesses.
10. Knowledge: The most important aspect of survival medicine is knowledge. It's important to have a basic understanding of anatomy, physiology and first aid to provide effective care in an emergency situation.

- Understanding the importance of mental and emotional well-being in survival

Maintaining mental and emotional well-being is crucial for survival in any situation. Here are some key principles to consider:

1. Positive Attitude: A positive attitude can make a big difference in a survival situation. It can help you stay motivated, focused and make better decisions.
2. Emotional Control: Being able to control your emotions is important in a survival situation. This includes being able to remain calm under stress, not panicking, and being able to think rationally.
3. Resilience: Resilience is the ability to bounce back from difficult situations. It's important to be resilient in a survival situation as it can help you to cope with the stress and uncertainty.
4. Support: Support from others can be a great help in a survival situation. This can include emotional support from friends, family, or a support group.
5. Mindfulness: Mindfulness is the practice of being aware of the present moment. It can help to reduce stress and improve focus, which can be beneficial in a survival situation.
6. Mental preparation: Having the right mindset and being mentally prepared for a survival situation can make a big difference. This can include learning survival skills, having a plan, and being aware of potential hazards.
7. Managing Stress: Stress can have a negative impact on your mental and emotional well-being. It's important to manage stress by taking care of yourself, getting enough sleep, and practicing stress-relieving techniques such as meditation or yoga.
8. Self-Care: Taking care of yourself is important for maintaining mental and emotional well-being. This can include eating nutritious food, getting enough sleep, staying hydrated and maintaining personal hygiene.
9. Coping Strategies: Coping strategies are tools and techniques that can help you to manage stress and difficult situations. These can include things like deep breathing, visualization, and positive self-talk.
10. Help-seeking: Knowing when to seek help is important. Mental and emotional health issues can have a significant impact on survival. If you are experiencing symptoms of mental or emotional distress, it's important to seek help from a healthcare professional.

Section 1: Advanced Survival Techniques

- Survival in extreme environments

Survival in extreme environments requires specific knowledge and skills to adapt to the unique challenges presented by each environment. In the desert, for example, survival strategies may focus on finding and conserving water, staying cool during the day, and staying warm at night. In the Arctic, survival may focus on staying warm, building shelter, and finding food. In the jungle, survival may focus on finding food and water, avoiding dangerous animals, and protecting against disease. It's also important to understand the local weather patterns, terrain, and vegetation. It's also important to have proper gear and equipment to help you survive in these environments. Additionally, having a good understanding of basic survival skills such as fire-making, shelter-building, and navigation is crucial. It's also important to be mentally and emotionally prepared for the challenges of survival in extreme environments.

- Survival in the wilderness

Survival in the wilderness requires a combination of knowledge, skills, and gear. Some important principles of wilderness survival include:

1. Prioritizing shelter: Finding or building a shelter to protect yourself from the elements should be one of your first priorities. This can include natural shelters like caves or overhangs, or man-made shelters like lean-tos or tarps.
2. Finding food and water: Knowing how to find and purify water, as well as how to forage for edible plants and hunt or fish for food, is essential for survival in the wilderness.
3. Building a fire: Fire can be used for warmth, cooking, and signaling for rescue. Knowing how to start a fire using natural materials is important.
4. Navigation: Being able to navigate using a map, compass, or natural

landmarks can help you find your way out of the wilderness.
5. First aid: Basic first aid skills, such as cleaning and dressing wounds, can help prevent infections and other health complications.
6. Mental and emotional well-being: Being mentally and emotionally prepared for the challenges of survival in the wilderness can help you stay calm and focused in a difficult situation.

- Survival in urban environments

Survival in urban environments can be different than survival in the wilderness, but it still requires knowledge, skills, and gear. Some important principles of urban survival include:

1. Finding shelter: In urban environments, finding shelter can be more challenging than in the wilderness. This can include finding a safe place to sleep, such as a park or abandoned building, or knowing how to make a shelter from urban debris.
2. Finding food and water: In an urban environment, finding food and water can be more challenging than in the wilderness. Knowing where to find food and water sources, such as dumpsters, food banks, and public fountains, is important.
3. Safety: In an urban environment, safety is a major concern. Knowing how to avoid danger, such as street crime, and how to defend yourself is important.
4. Navigation: Being able to navigate through an urban environment, using landmarks, public transportation or foot is essential.
5. First aid: Basic first aid skills, such as cleaning and dressing wounds, can help prevent infections and other health complications.
6. Mental and emotional well-being: Being mentally and emotionally prepared for the challenges of survival in an urban environment can help you stay calm and focused in a difficult situation.

- Survival in disaster scenarios

In a disaster scenario, the most important thing for survival is to stay calm and think clearly. Here are some key steps to follow:

1. Listen to local authorities and follow their instructions.
2. If you are in a disaster zone, try to find shelter immediately.
3. If you are in a building, stay inside and move to a safe area, such as a basement or an interior room away from windows.
4. If you are outside, try to find a sturdy structure to take shelter in.
5. Have emergency supplies on hand, such as food, water, a first aid kit, and a battery-powered radio.
6. Keep your phone charged and with you at all times, in case you need to call for help.
7. Be prepared to evacuate if necessary and know your escape routes.
8. Have a plan in place for reuniting with loved ones in case you get separated.
9. Stay informed about the disaster and be prepared for aftershocks or secondary hazards.
10. Help your neighbors, if it is safe to do so.

Remember, being prepared and having a plan in place can make a huge difference in a disaster scenario.

Section 2: Advanced Survival Medicine

- Identifying and treating injuries

Identifying and treating injuries in a disaster scenario is critical for survival. Here are some key steps to follow:

1. Assess the scene for safety before approaching any injured individuals.
2. Check for vital signs, such as breathing and pulse, and perform CPR if necessary.
3. Assess the nature and extent of injuries, including broken bones, cuts, burns, and head injuries.
4. Prioritize treatment based on the severity of the injury. Life-threatening injuries, such as severe bleeding, should be treated first.

5. Use basic first aid techniques to stop bleeding, such as applying pressure to the wound with a clean cloth.
6. Clean and dress wounds to prevent infection.
7. Immobilize any broken bones or sprains with a splint or sling.
8. Keep the injured person warm and comfortable, and monitor vital signs.
9. If possible, transport the injured person to a medical facility for further treatment.
10. Document the injuries and treatment provided, in case additional medical care is needed later.

It is important to note that, if you are not trained in first aid, it is better to call emergency services and wait for professional help.

- Identifying and treating illnesses

Identifying and treating illnesses in a disaster scenario can be challenging, but it is important for survival. Here are some key steps to follow:

1. Assess the individual's symptoms, such as fever, cough, shortness of breath, and stomach upset.
2. Check for vital signs, such as temperature, heart rate, and blood pressure.
3. Take note of any underlying health conditions or medications the individual may be taking.
4. Administer over-the-counter medications as appropriate, such as pain relievers and fever reducers.
5. Provide fluids and electrolytes to prevent dehydration.
6. Isolate anyone who appears to be contagious to prevent the spread of illness.
7. Seek medical attention if the individual's condition worsens or does not improve.
8. Keep good hygiene practices, such as washing your hands frequently and covering your mouth and nose when you cough or sneeze.
9. Monitor the individual's condition and document any changes or

treatment provided.

It is important to note that, if you are not trained in medical care, it is better to call emergency services and wait for professional help. Also, keeping a first aid kit with some basic medical supplies and a manual can be helpful in case of an emergency.

- Identifying and treating infections

Identifying and treating infections in a disaster scenario is important for preventing the spread of disease and ensuring the well-being of those affected. Here are some key steps to follow:

1. Observe for signs of infection, such as redness, warmth, swelling, and discharge from a wound or sore.
2. Clean the affected area with soap and water, or use an antiseptic solution if available.
3. Dress the wound with a clean bandage or dressing to keep it clean and dry.
4. Monitor the wound for signs of worsening or spreading infection, such as increasing redness, swelling, or discharge.
5. Administer antibiotics or other medication as prescribed by a medical professional.
6. Keep the individual comfortable and provide fluids to prevent dehydration.
7. Isolate anyone who appears to be contagious to prevent the spread of infection.
8. Seek medical attention if the individual's condition worsens or does not improve.
9. Keep good hygiene practices, such as washing your hands frequently and covering your mouth and nose when you cough or sneeze.

- Identifying and treating illnesses

Identifying and treating illnesses in a disaster scenario can be challenging, but it is important for survival. Here are some key steps to follow:

1. Be aware of the common illnesses that may occur after a disaster, such as respiratory infections, gastrointestinal illnesses, and skin infections.
2. Assess the individual's symptoms, such as fever, cough, shortness of breath, and stomach upset.
3. Check for vital signs, such as temperature, heart rate, and blood pressure.
4. Take note of any underlying health conditions or medications the individual may be taking.
5. Keep good hygiene practices, such as washing your hands frequently, covering your mouth and nose when you cough or sneeze, and properly disposing of any waste.
6. Administer over-the-counter medications as appropriate, such as pain relievers and fever reducers.
7. Provide fluids and electrolytes to prevent dehydration.
8. Isolate anyone who appears to be contagious to prevent the spread of illness.
9. Seek medical attention if the individual's condition worsens or does not improve.
10. Monitor the individual's condition and document any changes or treatment provided.

Section 3: Advanced Survival Psychology

- Understanding the importance of mental and emotional well-being in survival

Mental and emotional well-being is just as important as physical well-being in survival situations. Disasters can cause stress and trauma that can affect an individual's mental and emotional well-being, leading to symptoms such as anxiety, depression, and post-traumatic stress disorder (PTSD). Here are some key points to understand:

1. Acknowledge the emotional impact of a disaster on yourself and others. It is normal to feel a range of emotions, such as fear, sadness, and anger in the aftermath of a disaster.

2. Take care of yourself and others. Prioritize self-care activities such as getting enough sleep, eating well, and exercising.
3. Stay connected to friends, family, and community. Support from loved ones can provide a sense of security and stability during difficult times.
4. Seek professional help if you or someone you know is experiencing severe emotional distress. Trauma can have long-term effects on mental and emotional well-being, and professional help can provide support and guidance in recovery.
5. Be aware of the signs of stress and trauma, such as insomnia, nightmares, irritability, and difficulty concentrating.
6. Create a sense of normalcy, by keeping a routine and schedule, and engage in activities that you enjoy.
7. Be prepared to address the mental and emotional needs of children, who may have difficulty understanding and coping with a disaster.

In summary, maintaining mental and emotional well-being is crucial for survival in disaster scenarios. It is important to take care of oneself and others, stay connected, and seek professional help when necessary.

- Managing stress and anxiety

Managing stress and anxiety is important for survival in disaster scenarios as it can affect both physical and mental well-being. Here are some strategies for managing stress and anxiety:

1. Practice relaxation techniques, such as deep breathing, meditation, and yoga. These techniques can help to calm the body and mind and reduce feelings of anxiety.
2. Engage in physical activity, such as going for a walk, run or doing some exercise. Physical activity can help to release tension and improve mood.
3. Connect with others. Talking to friends, family or a therapist can help to alleviate stress and anxiety.
4. Keep a positive attitude and try to focus on the present moment.

Avoid dwelling on negative thoughts and try to maintain a sense of hope and optimism.
5. Take care of your physical health by getting enough sleep, eating well, and avoiding alcohol and drugs.
6. Seek professional help if you are experiencing severe symptoms of stress or anxiety such as panic attacks, persistent feelings of hopelessness, or difficulty functioning.
7. Create a plan for how to cope with stress and anxiety in case of future disaster scenarios.

- Building and maintaining a positive attitude

Building and maintaining a positive attitude is important for survival in disaster scenarios because it can help to reduce stress and anxiety, improve mood, and increase resilience. Here are some strategies for building and maintaining a positive attitude:

1. Focus on the present moment and try to stay in the present instead of dwelling on the past or worrying about the future.
2. Practice gratitude by focusing on the things you are thankful for in your life.
3. Engage in activities that you enjoy and that bring you a sense of pleasure and accomplishment.
4. Surround yourself with positive and supportive people who can help to boost your mood and provide a sense of security.
5. Set realistic and achievable goals for yourself, and work towards them. This can help to create a sense of purpose and accomplishment.
6. Try to find a sense of humor in difficult situations. A good laugh can help to improve mood and reduce stress.
7. Practice mindfulness and meditation to help stay focused and calm.
8. Try to maintain a healthy lifestyle and take care of your physical and mental well-being.
9. Learn from difficult experiences and try to see them as opportunities for growth and learning.

- Staying motivated and focused

Staying motivated and focused is important for survival in disaster scenarios because it can help to increase resilience, improve decision making, and increase the chances of survival. Here are some strategies for staying motivated and focused:

1. Set clear and achievable goals for yourself. Having a clear sense of direction and purpose can help to increase motivation and focus.
2. Prioritize self-care activities such as getting enough sleep, eating well, and exercising. Taking care of your physical and mental well-being can help to increase energy and focus.
3. Stay connected to friends, family, and community. Support from loved ones can provide a sense of security and stability, which can help to increase motivation and focus.
4. Keep a routine and schedule. Having a structure can help to increase focus and motivation.
5. Break down large tasks into smaller, more manageable steps. This can help to make the task feel less overwhelming and increase focus and motivation.
6. Take regular breaks to rest and recharge. Taking a break can help to prevent burnout and increase focus and motivation.
7. Reward yourself for achieving small goals along the way, it will motivate you to keep going.
8. Stay positive and focus on the things you can control, rather than dwelling on things that are out of your control.
9. Learn from mistakes and setbacks. Treat them as learning opportunities and try not to dwell on them.

IV. Conclusion

- **Summary of key takeaways**

In summary, survival in disaster scenarios involves several key components:

1. Being prepared by having an emergency plan and a survival kit.
2. Identifying and treating injuries, illnesses, and infections.
3. Understanding the importance of mental and emotional well-being and managing stress and anxiety.
4. Building and maintaining a positive attitude to reduce stress, improve mood, and increase resilience.
5. Staying motivated and focused by setting clear and achievable goals, prioritizing self-care, staying connected to loved ones, keeping a routine, and rewarding yourself along the way.

It's important to remember that these are ongoing processes and not always easy to maintain, especially in difficult situations. Seeking professional help if needed, and creating a plan for how to cope with stress and anxiety in case of future disaster scenarios are also important. Remember, being prepared and taking care of your physical and mental well-being can increase your chances of survival in disaster scenarios.

- Resources for further learning and practice

There are many resources available for further learning and practice when it comes to survival in disaster scenarios. Here are a few options:

1. Online courses: Websites such as Coursera, Udemy, and edX offer a wide variety of online courses on survival skills, emergency preparedness, and first aid.
2. Books: There are many books available on survival skills, emergency preparedness, and first aid. Some popular books include "The Survival Medicine Handbook," "The SAS Survival Handbook," and "Where There is No Doctor."
3. Websites: Websites such as the American Red Cross, the Federal

Emergency Management Agency (FEMA), and Ready.gov provide valuable information on emergency preparedness, including how to create a survival kit, develop an emergency plan, and respond to specific types of disasters.
4. Practice and training: Many organizations and companies offer training and practice opportunities for survival skills, emergency preparedness, and first aid. Some examples include the American Red Cross, the Community Emergency Response Team (CERT), and local fire departments.
5. Join a community: Join a community of preppers or survivalists, it can provide a great source of knowledge, advice, and support.

V. Appendices

- **List of materials and equipment needed for survival crafting**

Here is a list of materials and equipment that can be useful for survival crafting:

1. Knife or multi-tool: A sharp knife or multi-tool can be used for a variety of tasks, including cutting wood, preparing food, and making other tools.
2. Rope or cordage: Rope or cordage can be used for shelter building, setting up a clothesline, and creating a snare or trap.
3. Paracord: A strong and durable cord that can be unraveled for multiple uses, such as fishing line, suturing, or setting up a shelter.
4. Lighter or fire starter: A reliable fire starter is essential for survival, as fire can be used for cooking food, keeping warm, and signaling for help.
5. Water container: A water container, such as a water bottle or hydration bladder, can be used to store and transport water.
6. Water filter or purification tablets: A water filter or purification tablets can be used to make water safe to drink.
7. Compass and map: A compass and map can be used to navigate and find your way.
8. First aid kit: A basic first aid kit can be used to treat injuries and illnesses.
9. Tarp or plastic sheeting: A tarp or plastic sheeting can be used for shelter, rain protection, and as a ground cover.
10. Tent and sleeping bag: A tent and sleeping bag can provide shelter and warmth at night.
11. Survival blanket: A survival blanket can be used to retain heat and protect from the elements.
12. Headlamp or flashlight: A headlamp or flashlight can be used for lighting and signaling for help.
13. Blessing bag: A blessing bag is a bag that contains a variety of small items that can be useful

14. Fishing kits like fishing kits, hunting kits, trapping kits, fire starter kits, shelter kits, and signaling kits, etc.

- **Examples of specific survival scenarios and how to prepare for them**

1. Wilderness survival: If you're planning a camping or hiking trip in the wilderness, it's important to be prepared for the potential of getting lost or stranded. Some key ways to prepare for wilderness survival include:

- Bringing a map and compass and knowing how to use them.
- Bringing a survival kit that includes a knife, fire starter, and emergency shelter materials.
- Knowing how to find and purify water.
- Knowing how to signal for help.
- Knowing basic first aid skills.

1. Urban disaster: Urban disasters, such as earthquakes, tornadoes, and hurricanes, can happen unexpectedly and can cause widespread damage and disruption. To prepare for an urban disaster:

- Create an emergency plan for your family and make sure everyone knows what to do.
- Have emergency kits ready for your home, car, and workplace.
- Learn about emergency services in your area, such as where to find emergency shelters and evacuation routes.
- Keep important documents, such as ID, insurance, and important phone numbers in a waterproof bag
- Stay informed by listening to local news and following emergency services on social media.

1. Pandemics: In the case of pandemics, it's important to be prepared for the possibility of self-quarantine or isolation. To prepare for a pandemic:

- Stock up on non-perishable food and water, as well as basic medical supplies.
- Have a plan for how to stay in touch with loved ones and access necessary services remotely.
- Learn about the specific symptoms of the disease and how it spreads, so you can take appropriate precautions.
- Have a plan for how you will work or study from home if necessary.

This is not an exhaustive list of scenarios, but it gives an idea of the different types of scenarios that can happen and the different ways to prepare for them. Remember that being prepared is the key to survival, and it's important to always have a plan in place for different types of emergencies.

- **Glossary of terms used in the book**

Some common terms that are often used in the context of survival and emergency preparedness:

1. Bug-out bag (BOB): A bag containing essential items that can be used for survival in case of an emergency or disaster, such as food, water, shelter, and first aid supplies.
2. Fire starting: The process of creating a fire for warmth, cooking, and signaling for help.
3. Foraging: The process of finding and collecting wild food and resources.
4. Knots: A method of tying a rope or cordage in a specific way to hold or secure a load or to fasten things together.
5. Navigation: The process of finding your way and determining your location.
6. Purification: The process of making water safe to drink by removing harmful bacteria and other contaminants.
7. Shelter: A structure or place that provides protection from the elements, such as wind, rain, and sun.
8. Signaling: The process of using different methods to attract attention and communicate with others.

9. Survival: The ability to stay alive and cope with a difficult or dangerous situation.
10. Wilderness: An area of land that is mostly untouched by human development and is home to a wide variety of plants and animals.
11. First aid: The immediate care given to someone who is injured or ill before professional medical help can be obtained.
12. Mental and emotional well-being: The state of being mentally and emotionally healthy, and having the ability to cope with stress and difficult situations.
13. Trapping: Setting up traps to catch wild animals for food or as a means of protection.
14. Crafting: The process of making something by hand, usually by using natural materials, such as wood, leaves, and rocks.
15. Self-sufficiency: The ability to be independent and rely on oneself for survival, instead of relying on others or external resources.